LANGUAGE AND CULTURE IN CONFLICT

Problem-posing in the ESL Classroom

NINA WALLERSTEIN

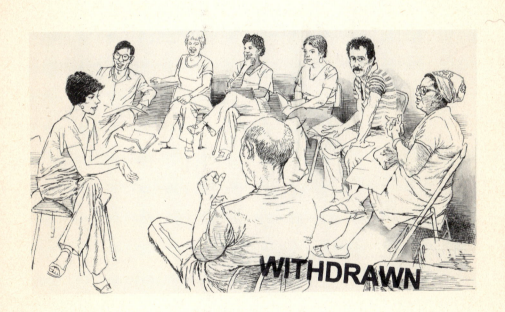

▲▼ **ADDISON-WESLEY PUBLISHING COMPANY**

Reading, Massachusetts • Menlo Park, California • Don Mills, Ontario
Amsterdam • London • Manila • Singapore • Sydney • Tokyo

Illustrations by Tom Leamon.

Photographs: p. 139, Cathy Cade; p. 9, 17, 42, 62, 70, 93, Robert Holmgren; p. 14, 70, 98, 137, Ken Light; p. 115 and 148, Deb Preusch.

Library of Congress Cataloging in Publication Data
Wallerstein, Nina, 1953–
    Language and Culture in Conflict:
    Problem-posing in the ESL Classroom.
    Bibliography: p.
    1. English language—Study and teaching—Foreign students. I. Title.
PE1128.A2W24   428.2′4′07   81-20641
ISBN 0-201-08290-X   AACR2

Credit: *Texas-Mexican Border Music Volume 2—Early Corridos* (Folk Lyric LP 9004).

ISBN 0-201-08290-X
ABCDEFGHIJ-AL-898765432

Contents

PREFACE

HOW IT ALL BEGAN

Part One

I WHO ARE THE STUDENTS?   3

Language and Cultural Problems of ESL Students   5
Social and Economic Problems of ESL Students   6
ESL Classes and the "American Way" of Life   8

II TEACHING APPROACH   11

Listening   12
Dialogue   15
Education as a Two-Way Process   15
Critical Thinking and Action   16
Problem-Posing   17
Codes   19
Chart Comparison of Problem-Posing
    and Other ESL Approaches   26

III TEACHING TECHNIQUES   27

    Codes   28
    Written Dialogues and Role-Plays   28
    Stories   29
    Pictures   30
    Puppets   31
    Tools for Dialogue   32
    Practice   32
    Conversation Circles   33
    Reading Comprehension Skills   33
    Writing Exercises   33
    Suggested Activities   34
    Active Techniques   34
    Beginners   35
    Problem-Posing Techniques for Beginners   35
    Team/Peer Teaching   36
    Foreign Language in the Classroom   37
    Bilingual Literacy   37

IV TECHNIQUES TO BE AVOIDED   39

    Situational Method   39

Part Two

USING THE STUDENT UNITS   45

    Writing a New Curriculum   48

Autobiography   50

    1 I'm New Here   52
    2 I Need Help   54
    3 My Family   56
    4 How Do You Feel?   58
    5 What Does She or He Look Like?   60
    6 Filling Out Papers   62
    7 What Do You Want to Be?   64
    8 Education Circle   66

The Family   68

    1 My Family   70
    2 At Home Every Day   72
    3 Housework   74
    4 Taking Care of Children   76

5 Teenagers   78
6 Rolando Galang's Story   80
7 Family Life   82
8 Going Out   84

Culture and Conflict   86

1 What Is Culture?   88
2 Getting Around   90
3 Languages in a Classroom   92
4 In a Fast-Food Restaurant   94
5 More Restaurants   96
6 Stereotypes   98
7 Cultural Neighborhoods   100
8 Culture and Family   102

Neighborhoods   104

1 My Home   106
2 My Neighborhood   108
3 I'm Lost   110
4 Renting a Home   112
5 Home Repairs   114
6 My Neighborhood in My Home Country   116
7 What's Happening in My Community?   118
8 Community Organizing   120

Immigration   122

1 Coming to the United States   126
2 Why Did You Come?   128
3 A Refugee's Story   130
4 My Hopes About the United States   132
5 Immigration Papers   134
6 Border Problems   136
7 My Rights   138
8 I'm a Citizen   140

Health   142

1 Calling the Clinic   144
2 At the Drugstore   146
3 How Do You Pay?   148
4 Neighborhood Health   150
5 Work Health   152
6 Medical Role-Plays   154
7 Stress at Work — Honju Na's Story   156
8 My Health   158

Work   160

1 What Is Your Job?   162
2 Work in the Home   164
3 Looking for Work   166
4 Job Application   168
5 Laid Off   170
6 Work in My Home Country   172
7 Women and Work   174
8 Safety in the Electronics Plant   176
9 Union   178

Money   180

1 Food Prices   182
2 Shopping in Different Countries   184
3 Shopping Complaint   186
4 Advertisements   188
5 At the Bank   190
6 Sending Money Home   192
7 Public Assistance   194
8 Taxes and Public Services   196

   A Brief Look at the U.S.:
      A Nation of Immigrants   198

Resources   201

   Materials for Classroom Use   201
   Educational Philosophy and Applications
      of Problem-Posing   202
   Background to Different Cultures   206
   References   209

Preface

"What do your students need to know?" the teacher trainer asks a group of English-as-a-Second-Language teachers gathered in the school lounge.

"English, of course, and how to survive here," one teacher answers.

"They already survive," a new Chicano teacher states. "I think they need English to make their lives better."

It is Saturday morning. Eight ESL teachers have requested a staff training session on the needs of their adult learners.

The trainer poses a new question, "What problems do your students have in learning English?"

"They don't have contact with English speakers outside of class."

"Mine just lack confidence. A lot of them are slow learners," exclaims a woman with technical authority.

"I don't think they're so slow," objects a young Cambodian teacher.

"I agree. They're just worried about many things—their families, their jobs," says an experienced Anglo teacher.

"They're certainly under stress, not knowing English. The ones from the refugee camps, especially, seem to be the saddest."

"That's true," states the Chicano, "I've found when they have family here they learn faster."

"So can you use their experiences to help them learn in class?" suggests the trainer.

"Oh, I don't want to waste class time."

"But they need to talk," says the Cambodian.

"Well, what words are easy to remember?" interjects the trainer.

"Oh, they remember the word, 'homesick,' or expressions like, 'What's the matter?' and 'I'm happy. I'm sad,'" says the older Anglo woman.

"Words about family—they're also easy to learn."

"What else works?" the trainer asks.

"I explain things in Spanish when it's necessary," responds the Chicano.

"I can't speak all my students' languages," says the Cambodian, *"but I let them help each other in their own language."*

"Not in my class," says the teacher with the technical view. *"I like a classroom with only English."*

"You know what's more important," the older woman says, *"My students want to talk about their lives in the countries they came from."*

"Yes, in my class, we celebrate students' holidays with food and songs."

"That's only part of their culture," the older teacher insists.

"What do you mean?" asks the teacher trainer. *"What culture do you teach in the classroom?"*

This dialogue among teachers is an example of the problem-posing approach which is the focus of this book. The dialogue contains topics and problems familiar to many teachers: the worries and stress that students bring with them to class, the questions of students maintaining their language and culture, and the creative use of students' feelings and experiences to enhance English learning.

Just as teachers learn from each other in dialogues like these, students and teachers can be co-learners in the ESL classroom. "It is important, indeed indispensable, that you be convinced that each meeting with your group will leave you and its members enriched" (Freire 1971).

How It All Began

This book's philosophy and curriculum materials had their beginnings in 1973, when I helped organize a community education project in a Spanish-speaking neighborhood of San Jose, California. Under the auspices of the Metropolitan Adult Education District, we had a year-long state education grant to develop an adult education program with residents of this under-served community. Working *with* residents, we believed, would create a more effective program than if we had decided the courses beforehand.

When I started, I knew very little about the educational method called problem-posing. I knew that Freire had initiated a highly successful nation-wide literacy program for Brazilian slumdwellers in the early 1960s. I knew also that his ideas had been catalysts for education programs worldwide. I was not sure, however, how a "Freire" approach could apply to low-income adult education students in the United States. During the year, I learned how this approach could enliven classroom interaction and student learning, while conveying a sense of community among students and teachers.

True to a Freire approach, we started the program by listening. Our team of five to seven persons conducted research for two months on the needs or "themes" of the community before launching into adult education classes. We talked to neighbors, met with church and community groups, observed people in parks, and visited social service agencies. Many of the themes we uncovered became the core of our ESL curriculum. Our team consisted of two Chicanos and two Anglos from the community, and three Anglos who came from the outside—all bilingual; two of us outsiders moved into the community before starting work.

I came to the project after studying community education at the University of California. I had learned Spanish early during childhood summers in Mexico. Previously, I had worked as a community organizer and student teacher, but this was my first opportunity to work with adults who were creating their own educational program.

After repeatedly hearing residents declare their need for English, four of us decided to set up a free, open-entry, open-exit English as a Second Language class. Other team members went on to set up a church discussion group, a women's group, and community workshops. To begin the class, we faced the difficult task of recruiting adult students (particularly women or older people who traditionally would stay at home) who had not been to school for many, many years. We needed to make the class as accessible as possible, and to provide support services.

Searching the area, we decided to hold class in an unused community room of a public housing project. There we had a ready student population with the embryo of a unified community. We recruited students by walking door-to-door, in and outside of the project, and talking in Spanish about the class. We contacted community leaders and posted announcements in stores and welfare offices. We also recruited potential students at places (and times) where non-English speakers first come into contact with Anglo culture. We realized that many women discover their need for English as their children enter kindergarten; children's teachers therefore were a source of referral.

Our enrollment the first week easily reached thirty people, and we maintained a daily attendance of over fifteen. We found continuous recruitment necessary among a population who had never attended school in the U.S. and who had everyday problems that inhibited daily attendance. Other demands in their lives often took precedence: sick children or the seasonal low-paid jobs most worked in—construction, cannery work, or farm labor.

We also discovered the importance of childcare and transportation to maintain enrollment, for the majority of people couldn't afford them. We set up bilingual drop-in childcare in a room nearby where parents could leave their children before class.

The majority of ESL students came from Mexico and Central America, with a few from Portugal. The age span was 16–70 years old with twice as many women as men. (One of our successes was in encouraging women to attend.) Most of our students were first-generation immigrants who had lived in the United States for the past 5–15 years. Despite having U.S.-born children, the students felt strong attachments to their home countries. They wanted their children to learn Spanish but did not care to return to Mexico themselves. With family members in two countries, people felt mixed loyalties. Most of the women had not actively decided to immigrate, but had followed their husbands, who had immigrated for work. The issue of men's and women's roles emerged in lively class discussions.

Towards the end of the year, we had an influx of single, young, new immigrants who did not experience double identities. With these two distinct groups, our discussions about culture and conflict became quite heated as we argued the validity of a bicultural identity versus a purely Mexican identification.

After recruiting students, we wondered how to create a problem-posing curriculum that built on issues in students' lives and encouraged active dialogue in class. We arranged the chairs in a circle to establish a relaxed atmosphere for equal participation. Our first lessons were devoted to asking autobiographical questions about students' families, culture, work, and what they liked and did not like about the U.S. We also explored students' needs and feelings about learning English. "Where do you speak English now?" we asked. "What do your children speak? Where do you need English?" Answers to these many questions gave us information on our students' English proficiencies and on themes for the year's curriculum. We wrote dialogues on situations where students needed English, on daily life issues, and on people's mixed feelings about learning English and living in the United States.

Other themes concerning community issues and events emerged. In the middle of the year, tenants at the housing project called a strike against management for rent increases and lack of maintenance. One of our students co-chaired the tenants' association, and he talked in class about the issues affecting half of the class members. To increase students' contacts with the Anglo world, we invited speakers to talk of community resources, or took field trips out of the class.

Naturally, the class had its share of problems and challenges. Some were found in all adult classes; some were particular to our class. The first problem will doubtless be familiar: attendance fluctuated. In addition to family or employment pressures, adult students often have high expectations for immediate, applicable learning. If their expectations are not met, they often express dissatisfaction by dropping out. Adults from other cultures will often defer to authority. In the language classroom, the teacher represents authority, and students hesitate to criticize or try to change the class. They simply stop coming.

The second problem we had to resolve, therefore, was how to solicit student opinions about the class or curriculum. We knew we could have evaluated the class without the students' input: which techniques worked well or poorly; which lesson plans should be repeated, dropped, or modified. But involving students in directing the class was one of our primary goals.

To involve students, we first had to ask ourselves some hard questions. What were our goals of teaching? What did we want students to learn? And what did we want to learn from our students (about our teaching and about ourselves)? When we started, candid statements of students' preferences were extremely difficult to elicit. What *did* they like best? Due to politeness or cultural strictures many people hesitated to give negative comments. Yet when they realized we often followed their suggestions, students began to give straightforward answers.

The third major problem was how to hold discussions on important issues with limited-English-speaking students. In giving workshops, I am often asked, "How can I do problem-posing when my students barely speak?"

In San Jose, we attempted various solutions. As our class was multi-level, we could separate the intermediate students into a smaller group and direct discussions with them through the questioning problem-posing process (see TEACHING APPROACH). At times, we allowed the whole group to shift into Spanish when the discussion became heated, and/or when people became frustrated with their English-speaking ability. (In multi-lingual classes, of course, bilingual discussions would be impossible.)

We also found beginners could follow most of the written dialogues and understand critical issues when the conversations were acted out in front of the class. By listening for students' laughter, we easily evaluated how much they understood—especially when the more advanced students transformed the role-plays with their own surprising endings. The physical movements of the acting gave a context to the new vocabulary and reinforced the students' learning. Although beginners could not pursue full discussions, we felt we *had* created a problem-posing environment. We taught beginning students enough vocabulary to ask each other questions; this created mutual learning and built conversation skills among students.

Our fourth and most important problem in developing this Freire-based program was that funding from the state only lasted one year, yet the issues in our curriculum (and the consequences for our students) lasted far longer than one year. A problem-posing process implies a serious and long-term commitment to developing critical thinking skills and acting on issues raised in class. At the end of the year's work, we felt we *had* accomplished some of the original goals. We had been able to develop a model adult education program established with community members. We had designed a curriculum that gave students the tools and confidence for thinking critically and for taking actions in their lives. And we, the teachers, had been enriched by the experience.

ACKNOWLEDGEMENTS

I wish to express my appreciation to all the people who supported my ideas and the writing of this book. My initial thanks go to John McFadden and Esther Stone who gave me my first opportunity to work in a Paulo Freire participatory education project in San Jose, California. My fellow team members on the project, Janice Baker, Patricia Lamborn, and Mario Castro were helpful in the early draft of the manuscript. I would particularly like to thank Pia Moriarty for her invaluable co-partnership in the development of the ideas and materials presented in this book.

This book could not have been written without my trying out the ideas in my own classrooms. I owe special appreciation therefore to the patience of all my students from whom I learn as I continue to teach.

Much work and many hands go into the publishing of a book. For indepth editing, I thank Nancy Guinn, David Dunaway, and John Berger who helped me rethink difficult passages. For preparation of the manuscript, I owe thanks to Linda Gaede and to the editorial and production staff of Addison-Wesley. For the illustrations and photographs, I thank Ken Light, Cathy Cade, Robert Holmgren, Deb Preusch and Tom Leamon. A special thank you to my friends and fellow teachers who gave me helpful suggestions and field-tested the materials, in particular Margit Birge, Cynthia Brown, Camy Condon, Linda Francois, Lila Gonzalez, Mark Lowe, Martin Manley, and Judith Wallerstein.

Finally, I offer thanks to my community of friends, Cooperative Camp members, and family for their understanding in the last difficult months of writing, and to David Dunaway, whose love and faith helped me to reach the end.

I hope this book will encourage an exchange of ideas and material from other teachers involved in similar programs or curriculum development. I would welcome any comments from people as they read, try out units, and incorporate problem-posing into their own teaching.

Albuquerque, NM   Nina Wallerstein
1982

PART ONE

Chapter 1

Who Are the Students?

My name is Gloria Armez. I was born in Humacao, Puerto Rico. I was eight when I moved to San Juan with my sister. I liked Humacao better. It's smaller and I knew a lot of people there.

I worked as a cashier part-time in Franklins, an American store. Many of the stores were American. I was paid 40¢ an hour. It is hard to find work there. There was more work before the U.S. took a lot of land.

Then I got married. In February 1966, we moved to New York. My husband came to find work. Now he works as a janitor. I work as a cashier in a Spanish store. What's different?

This story was written by an ESL student who sums up in simple, yet vivid English her feelings about immigrating and life in the United States. *Language and Culture in Conflict* demonstrates how people's lives can be the basis for teaching English, using the problem-posing approach developed by the Brazilian, Paulo Freire. Freire began his literacy curriculum with students' lives and their fatalistic attitude that they could never effect change. Using carefully selected words and pictures that presented the problems and potential in their lives, he motivated students to analyze their experience—why they lived in slums, why others lived better, and what they could do about their problems (Freire 1973).

Problem-posing is based on the premise that education starts with issues in people's lives and, through dialogue, encourages students to develop a *critical* view of their lives and the ways to *act* to enhance their self-esteem, and improve their lives.

3

This approach is not limited to use in literacy programs. It is particularly well-suited to adult ESL classrooms. It may be equally valuable in A.B.E., G.E.D., or other community adult classes. Like the population Freire worked with, the majority of ESL students come from a low socio-economic background. Most have had little formal education. They experience many situations in the U.S. which make them feel vulnerable and inadequate. Even if they possess technical skills, ESL students have limited access to jobs. They are often humiliated for their "accent" and blame themselves for not succeeding in America.

These problems (with life in the United States) affect students' self-images; they often create difficulties in learning English. How often have teachers heard students say, "I'm dumb. I just can't learn English. I come to class every semester and look at me."

Problem-posing uses students' experiences and their cultural and personal strengths to try to resolve the problems in their everyday lives. Starting with emotionally charged topics, students invest more of themselves in talking and using their English, both inside and outside the classroom. One lesson in my class—about being sick and not having a private physician—led students to act out phone calls to a clinic, requesting appointments from the receptionist who had trouble understanding the students' English. Laughter accompanied language practice as students held their heads in their hands, limped around the room, and kept saying, "What? what?" Not only did everyone learn the target vocabulary, but after the roleplay, the class discussed (in animated yet fractured English) frustrations of all involved—the receptionist and the patient, students' feelings of not speaking English well, the difficulties in getting good medical care, and the importance of improving the interactions.

The first step in problem-posing for us, as teachers, is to *listen* to our students and learn about their problems and strengths. Anyone struggling with a different language or culture experiences anxieties, a form of "culture shock" with "language shock" as an integral ingredient. People often become disoriented, find social encounters threatening, and fear making mistakes (Smalley 1963). As one Vietnamese student poignantly said, "I don't understand English. For me, it's like a duck trying to talk to a chicken."

LANGUAGE AND CULTURAL PROBLEMS OF ESL STUDENTS

Not knowing English isolates people, for language is more than a means of communication—it's a reflection of culture. Language is a principal source of group identity and the transmission of that identity to the children. As people live in the United States and learn English, they simultaneously reframe their culture and absorb new cultural and social underpinnings.

Every culture is extraordinarily complex and subtle. A culture is defined, in part, by behavior, speech and gestures, art, music, family, socio-economic systems, values—and more. Culture is often mistaken for the "fine art" that appears in museums; some include the "folk art" which reflects a people's traditions and handicraft work. Yet both these notions obscure culture, by separating it from people's daily activities and livelihood. The social and economic conditions of craftwork, for instance, are often invisible. Tourists will travel into villages and buy ceramic pottery cheaply, little thinking about their use or the labor that produced the pots. A culture therefore includes how people labor, create, and make life choices.

When people come to the U.S., they've made a life-choice to seek their living and their survival away from their native culture. In fact, refugees and immigrants may have much to teach us about survival skills. To do well in the U.S., they need English; yet for their emotional and social stability, the new arrivals also need to preserve their cultural integrity.

Students of ESL, whether immigrants or native-born, face pressures to assimilate into one dominant culture. Although the melting pot theory no longer predominates within American society, many ESL students find that its replacement—cultural pluralism—is also a myth. Minorities are often expected to absorb Anglo culture (and language) while many Anglo-Americans learn and understand very little about the cultures of the minority groups.

How do these interactions between students' cultures and the dominant Anglo culture shape teaching in our classrooms? To begin with, when we teach a second language, we are introducing different cultural expectations and communicative styles. Unfortunately, there is potential for miscommunication on both sides. Greetings in English, for example, do not contain the subtleties of address found in other languages that convey formality, intimacy, or respect.

Non-verbal language can also cause cultural miscommunication. People may feel "out of sync" in another culture—they seem to be talking too loud or standing too close (Hall 1976). Complete misunderstandings can occur. Many Indochinese students, for example, will nod yes to the teacher's questions whether they understand or not. Teachers may not realize that the nod could be out of politeness and not out of understanding.

We must be sensitive to our students' cultural distinctions and values. In class, as we teach the appropriate manner to get around in the dominant culture, we (and our students) can learn the appropriate ways to act in other cultures. We can contribute to a culturally pluralistic attitude that acknowledges cultural communities in the U.S.

SOCIAL AND ECONOMIC
PROBLEMS OF ESL STUDENTS

If cultural pluralism is rare, socio-economic pluralism is even rarer. Many ESL students find Anglo-American society threatening. Whether recent immigrants entering a new environment or second-generation citizens, these students are limited by economic and educational inequalities. Many do not have, or know *how* to have, the opportunity to become professionals. Immigrants and minorities often end up taking the low-paying jobs that other Americans don't want.

Before they arrive and live in the U.S., many immigrants dream of a better life here (if not for them, then for their children). They come for many different reasons—religious, political, economic, social, voluntary or involuntary—but all hope to improve their lives and to support any family back home. They are taking a risk and have high expectations. Some achieve their hopes, yet many find life difficult. Their hopes and disillusionments are aptly portrayed in a Mexican corrido, "El Lavaplatos" (The Dishwasher).

> "I dreamed in my youth
> of being a movie star
> And one of those days I came
> to visit Hollywood."

> (The young man came without paying immigration and worked on the railroad track, picked tomatoes, gathered beets, laid cement, then thought he was better off washing dishes.)

"It is the decent work
done by many Chicanos
Although with the hot water,
the hands swell a little."

(The immigrant in the song got tired of dishwashing and lost his dreams
of success in the U.S.)

"Goodbye dreams of my life,
goodbye movie stars,
I am going back to my beloved homeland,
much poorer than when I came."

The results of economic, cultural, and linguistic discrimination are far-
reaching and complex for ESL students. While many students express
legitimate anger at discrimination, others blame themselves because of their
inability to speak English. Such feelings can create a negative acculturation
and perpetuate the cultural conflicts of living in the United States. Instead of
positive or creative adaptations that incorporate elements of both cultures,
ESL students may find themselves rejecting either American culture or
their own. Some students leave the U.S. after many years.

My life is a real story, especially here in the U.S. where they drive me crazy from working so much. I don't like the customs of this country anyhow. Although my children are grown up, I don't want *their* children to be pocho. We're going back to Mexico (Gamio 1971).

Some immigrants want to be "Americanized" and forget their heritage. Often, their children want to be Americanized and refuse to speak the native language as an act of rebellion. For the most part, however, ESL students resent their children's resistance to speaking the native language and want to preserve their culture.

With time, the majority of ESL students begin to synthesize a new identity combining their native cultures and U.S. culture. Often they feel a dual emotional citizenship and travel back and forth, if money and politics permit. Many choose to live in distinct cultural neighborhoods in hopes that their children will speak their native languages. Within these neighborhoods, some people live a restricted existence, never venturing out of their language ghettos. Nevertheless, these neighborhoods are distinctly American, and most residents, especially the children, emerge with a bicultural identity. Their attachments to their cultures or a mixed culture remain strong. "Puerto Ricans living in the U.S. don't speak Spanish. They mix in English. They speak Spanglish," one student related.

ESL CLASSES AND THE "AMERICAN WAY" OF LIFE

Americanization

CITIZENSHIP, PREPARATION FOR   A review of United States Government structure for those preparing for citizenship examination.

ENGLISH AS A SECOND LANGUAGE   The English as a Second Language (ESL) courses are designed to provide language immersion that attempts to enable a non-English speaker to function in an English-speaking environment as quickly as possible. ESL is often called survival English. Citizens, permanent residents and refugees pay no fee for ESL classes. (Berkeley . . . Adult School, Berkeley, California)

For ESL students, learning English can begin the process of gaining control in their lives: getting a job, having access to needed services. At the same time, however, learning English creates conflicts when people don't want to forsake their own culture and language. ESL classes can symbolize an assimilation students both desire and fear.

The classroom situation therefore re-enacts the conflicts experienced in students' daily exposure to Anglo society, and implicitly becomes a *focus* of cultural conflict. Despite well-meaning teachers, these conflicts (and students' fears of losing their own language) inhibit language learning inside and outside the classroom. The sense of language is particularly sensitive for parents who want their children to share their culture.

Unfortunately, much of traditional ESL instruction ignores students' bilingual/bicultural identities. The curriculum is often isolated from the problems students confront daily. Even multicultural materials are sometimes oriented towards becoming Anglo. Students are often asked to identify with a stereotypic American nuclear family unit: the men work, and the women take care of the house and children. Many ESL students, however, come from extended families where both parents work in low-paid jobs. The multicultural attempts of schools can also portray a romanticized view of culture as festivals, crafts, and dances. Curriculum on Latin America, for example, has offered corn and beans as typical "quaint" food. Though these foods provide a complete protein meal, this diet is the product of poverty, of people lacking a choice of whether or not to eat meat.

How, then, can we best teach English and avoid diminishing students' culture and self-esteem? Students vitally need English for emergencies, for communication with other people, for their children. As one student wrote, "I have three children, and they need help of me." Students need to develop self-confidence to improve their language interactions in dealing with bureaucracies or authorities. A student expressed this well: "I come to class to learn how to defend myself in English."

√ The problem-posing approach takes these conflicts—the difficulties students have in living in the U.S., their feelings of vulnerability, and their desire to learn English while maintaining their own culture—as the center of the curriculum. Written dialogues and role-plays based on problem situations generate motivational energy, and students are inspired to work hard to speak English. They also reduce their anxieties by enacting troublesome situations, changing the plots, and finding more satisfying endings.

√ Problem-posing allows students and teachers to explore life situations, create hope about change, and use their imaginations to build the link between classroom English and the community. ESL students are making a serious commitment. A problem-posing approach offers them a chance to redefine their culture and gain mastery over their lives. In Brazil, Paulo Freire's literacy education gave people an oral and written voice to "name" their problems and become active members of society. It was discovered that people didn't only learn to read and write, but they read and wrote to learn.

For our ESL students, we may rephrase this: "Our students don't just need to learn English; they need English so they can *learn*."

In this view, the goals of teaching English become more comprehensive: to give people the skills to cope better in the U.S.—and, in fact, to do more than cope—to take risks by asking for what they want. In the classroom, this means a language of action to help students seek alternatives. Curriculum based on students' cultures reaffirms their dignity and the strengths they already have. The classroom becomes an exciting and relaxed place for students and teachers to exchange life experiences and promote cross-cultural communication. As people learn to speak, read, and write English, they will name their *"worlds"* not just the *"words"* (Freire, 1970).

Chapter 2

Teaching Approach

"Adult education should have as one of its main tasks to invite people to believe in themselves. It should invite people to believe that they have knowledge" (Freire 1973 *Convergence*).

As previously stated, the problem-posing approach comes from the work of Brazilian educator Paulo Freire, author of *Pedagogy of the Oppressed*. Born in Brazil's impoverished Northeast to a lower middle-class family, Freire eventually completed his college and legal degrees. He gave up his law practice in the late forties to set up literacy classes in factories. As a professor of education at the University of Recife, the largest city in the Northeast, he coordinated a Church-sponsored adult education program and developed his "dialogue" approach with slumdwellers and peasants. In 1963, he became coordinator of the National Literacy Program, bringing basic education to tens of thousands throughout Brazil.

Freire encouraged people to view themselves as active creators of culture, not passive recipients of history. He believed people create and recreate their culture as they earn a living, pass on values, and interact in social groups. By encouraging students to reflect on their role as creators, Freire challenged his students to believe in themselves as agents of change. "Once (the students) perceive that their music has as much culture as the music of Beethoven, they can begin to break down their dimensions of inferiority. It is this inferiority which prevents them from participating in the true creation of their society" (Freire 1973 *Convergence*). This process, described in *Education for Critical Consciousness*, enabled his adult students to read and write after only six weeks of study, thus making them active members of society by gaining the right to vote (Freire 1973).

Exiled from Brazil in 1964 after the military takeover, Freire went to Chile until 1968, then taught for a year as a visiting professor at Harvard. From 1970-1979 he worked as director of the Office of Education for the World Council of Churches in Geneva. In 1979, Freire returned to Brazil. His ideas have been the catalyst for many adult education and community development programs both in the third world and in industrialized nations.

Paulo Freire's phonetic literacy method is not directly applicable to the United States. His students were a homogeneous group; ESL students come from diverse backgrounds. Freire himself recognizes that "experiments cannot be transplanted, they must be reinvented" (Freire 1978). Yet with creative reinventions, Freire's central theme does apply to our classrooms. Education should compel people to analyze and challenge those forces in society which keep them passive. This theme is based on the premise that education is not neutral and does not take place in a vacuum outside society. It either prepares people to accept or to challenge their life situations.

The Freire concepts and methods that reinforce this philosophy are divided into three stages: *Listening*, which begins before teaching; *Dialogue*, which takes place in class; and *Action*, which extends to consequences outside the classroom. *Dialogue* leads to *Action* as teachers and students explore *Education as a Two-Way Process*, *Critical Thinking*, *Problem-posing*, and *Codes*.

LISTENING

To develop a problem-posing curriculum, we need to know about our students, their cultural traditions, their strengths in starting a new life, and their daily concerns. But how do we learn about (and from) our students if we don't speak their languages? We can begin this process by listening.

Listening simply means employing our observational skills with a systematic approach similar to anthropological fieldwork. "Problem-posing" listening also assumes that everyone—students and teachers—can participate on an ongoing basis. Teachers do not have to work alone to discover their students' issues. Cross-cultural understandings actually emerge more easily out of an interaction of students and teachers. People can recognize each other's cultural biases and learn to avoid misinterpreting each other.

As teachers, we carefully listen to our students' conversations and interactions. To create a curriculum tailored to students and their daily concerns, we need to listen systematically. Effective listening takes time, as does getting to know people. But the time is well spent, and the process can begin at any time by using our basic sense of watching, listening and intuiting.

1. How Can We Listen/Observe Effectively?

Look for verbal and non-verbal clues, and for individual and environmental factors.

Observation is a valuable skill, especially when teachers don't speak the students' languages. Consider what a careful observer can discover about the learning styles of Cantonese students (ethnic Chinese from Vietnam) versus those of Laotian (including Mien) students.

Cantonese students tend to sit upright, focus on the teacher, and repeat individually or as a group after the teacher. Laotian students are strikingly different. They tend to lean toward each other, talk under their breath as they point out the lessons to their neighbors and laugh at (and with) each other's attempts to speak English. Observing the two classrooms demonstrates the importance of teachers having sensitivity to their students' cultural styles. With these sensitivities, teachers may be able to create a comfortable atmosphere congruent with their students' expectations.

In the Classroom:

Watch students' interaction—how they greet each other, say goodbye, show respect, touch each other, express pleasure, dismay, or other feelings.

Observe body language in learning—whether they work together or alone, sit rigidly or lean towards each other, praise each other or compete.

Observe students' actions—what they reveal about priorities or problems. For instance, many Indochinese students frequently miss class due to illness. Health care could then be a major discussion issue in a class of refugees.

Ask students to share objects from their culture (kitchen implements, handicrafts, handmade household tools, clothes, anything they have made).

Listen for informal conversations held during the break or before and after class. These talks can often be the richest source of information.

Create curriculum about everyday activities—students' home and family life (where do family members live? where do students feel at home?), their neighborhood life (who do they know in the community? do they interact with other cultural/ethnic groups?), and their work life (what do they like and not like? how is work different in their home country?)

In the Community:

Walk through students' neighborhoods, school and work environs and *take photographs* to bring back to class. Be systematic—observe at the same time for a few days, or at the same place at different times, and record impressions.

Walk with students through their neighborhoods or around the school. Through fieldtrips and walks, students' use of English in the community will increase. If possible, have students take photographs.

Draw maps of houses and services in the neighborhoods. This can be a class exercise: have students draw stores, parks, bus stops, or social places important in their lives.

Ask people on the street as well as community workers about issues in the community. Have *students conduct interviews*, and bring results and their own observations to class.

In Students' Homes:

Observe students' lives outside of class—their living conditions, their material expressions of culture, their manner of treating the teacher as an honored guest. Access to students' homes is a privilege and provides great opportunities to learn more about their lives.

2. What Are the Cultural Attributes to Observe?

Look for cultural differences and expressions of group identity.

Times of Cultural Transmission

Observe social rites including rituals of becoming an adult, weddings, or baby showers. Invitations to these experiences are again a privilege.

Observe child-raising practices and parents' expectations for children's behavior. Students can discuss the differences between child-rearing in their culture and in the U.S. They can also tell childhood stories.

Times of Cultural Preservation

Attend (or have schools sponsor) *celebrations* from students' culture and history. Learn about the foods, dress, rituals, and values.

Ask students about their home country—what they used to do, whether they want to return, what values they want to retain, for themselves and for their children.

Times of Cultural Disruption

Ask students about their immigration—how they felt when they left, why and how they came, what they expected, how they feel now about their lives.

Have students compare their lives in the two countries in different arenas: health, work, family, education, etc.

3. How Can We Verify What We Hear?

This is ultimately the most important step. Cross-cultural understanding comes in what we as teachers observe, transform into curriculum, and then receive in feedback from our students. A Freire process entails constant listening for students' responses to ensure our own learning and the relevance of the curriculum for each class.

A dialogue about problems in obtaining immigration papers, for example, may reflect the concerns of a Latin American student but not apply to the problems of Indochinese refugees. Students' responses to the curriculum will help us as teachers adapt or improve the lessons. The responses may also add information that we did not or could not understand when first observing. A map of a neighborhood drawn by a teacher, for example, could not possibly include information on who has just moved in or *why* a neighbor built a fence.

In sum, listening helps select the key concerns of students to shape into culturally sensitive lessons.

DIALOGUE

To Freire, dialogue means much more than conversation; it is an exchange between everyone in a class, student to student and teacher to student. The term involves *action*—students initiate discussions, lessons, and activities to fulfill their educational needs.

Dialogue differs from the traditional lecture and seminar methods where the teacher determines the scope of discussion and students remain passive objects of learning. A Freire approach to dialogue assumes students equally determine classroom interaction. As adults, they bring their concerns and personal agendas to class. These concerns determine what's important to discuss.

In an ABE/ESL class, this dialogue assumes many forms. In curriculum content, students introduce their personal backgrounds, their needs for education, their cultural differences with each other and with Anglo-America, and the problems they confront daily. In classroom dynamics, students participate in discussion circles, divide into small groups or pairs for structured peer teaching, or learn directly from the teacher. In attitudes, students and teachers communicate as co-learners.

Teaching creatively with the dialogue approach makes ESL more than just learning a new language. As students exercise control within the classroom by choosing which issues are crucial, they will gain confidence to use English and to make changes in their lives outside of school.

EDUCATION AS A TWO-WAY PROCESS

The use of dialogue challenges the traditional role of a teacher. Rather than presenting ourselves as omniscient, we participate in a two-way process, learning alongside our students about each others' lives and cultures. For adult students, the tensions involved in learning ease as teachers become known as real people. Teachers can also relax their lecturing or performance role. As teachers and students get to know each other, they will be freer to exchange criticisms or appreciative remarks. Students will discuss their dissatisfactions more openly as well as give needed encouragement to others.

Teachers will also be more personal as they emphasize their students' progress to lessen the normal frustrations in learning a new language.

As students talk about their lives, the classroom becomes a place of learning and excitement for teachers. Many ESL teachers have not had the opportunity to travel in students' home countries or interact with students in their cultural communities within the U.S. Many teachers are not fluent in the students' language, and lack in-depth knowledge about their culture. Using dialogue and a multicultural curriculum established in partnership can stimulate learning and mutual understanding.

CRITICAL THINKING AND ACTION

The goal of the dialogue approach is to encourage critical thinking about the world. By discussing their personal experiences students can uncover the social pressures which affect them as members of an ethnic group. A critical view does *not* imply negative thinking. Critical thinking builds on the hopes that students have for a better life. Students have already experienced change in their lives by immigrating, and are searching for other changes in the U.S. Analyzing U.S. society enables students to adopt a positive stance towards the change they want, in their personal lives or with their community. Communication with immigrants, ethnic groups and Anglo-Americans can increase as people share their culture and move beyond stereotypes that separate groups in America.

Critical thinking in the classroom does not take place randomly; a teacher promotes inquiry by posing questions and providing information to lead the discussion into a larger social context. Students evaluate the forces that exert control on their lives. Layoffs, racism on the job, cultural discrimination, inflation, education, family—these forces limit their choices of how they live. Critical thinking begins when people make the connections between their individual lives and social conditions. It ends one step beyond perception—towards the *action* people take to regain control over social structures detrimental to their lives.

Action and change do not come easily. Many adult English students are unused to criticizing institutions or demanding reforms. They might be unhappy that their children's school system has no bilingual program, for example, but feel they do not have the privilege or right to demand such programs.

Action *can* begin in the classroom. The first step towards action is to have students reflect on their common experience. Sometimes their only shared experience is what happens in the classroom. Why are they studying? What do they learn in the classroom? What can they learn from their fellow students? What do they learn *outside* of the classroom? These discussions can elicit criticisms or suggestions for better teaching. If the atmosphere allows students to say what they think, they will have made a step towards control in one aspect of their lives.

Curriculum can also reflect students' common experiences outside of the classroom, their stories and life problems. As students identify shared issues, they may gain insight into actions to better their situations. To encourage these insights, the lesson materials themselves must include a language of action. Many ESL texts teach a language of survival or of expressing an opinion or purpose. Few, however, teach language that goes beyond identifying or accepting a situation—language that leads toward empowerment. A Freire approach considers language of action central to learning English. Lessons on neighborhood issues such as barking dogs, inadequate city services, or no heating, for example, could expand to include language about block organizing or tenants' rights. Learning language can initiate small steps towards change. Students need to be successful taking a small risk in order to gain confidence for larger ones.

Sometimes, the school setting will provide enough of a community for group student actions or programs. Students in closed-entry semester or year-long courses develop a sense of community where they may follow through on issues raised in the classroom. Or if the school creates a community providing services or a social center (like many Indochinese centers), students can get involved in self-help or collective programs. Some school centers have created farmers' food markets, selling cooperatives (i.e. the Hmong Pan Dau sales), women's groups, or parent-assisted childcare centers. When students are ready, other actions can take place within language-learning—writing letters to congressional representatives, or writing and circulating petitions, organizing neighborhood cleanups—whatever actions are important to the students.

PROBLEM-POSING √

Problem-posing is the tool for developing critical thinking. It is an inductive questioning process that structures dialogue in the classroom. Teachers formulate questions to encourage students to make their own conclusions about society's values and pressures. The problem-posing method draws out students' shared experiences of society.

Problem-posing, as stated earlier, begins by listening for students' issues. Based on the listening, teachers then select and present the familiar situations back to the students in a codified form: a photograph, a written dialogue, a story, or a drawing (See *Codes*). Each situation contains personal and social conflicts which are emotionally charged for students. Teachers ask a series of inductive questions which move the discussion of the situation from the concrete to a more analytic level. The problem-posing process directs students to name the problem, understand how it applies to them, determine the causes of the problem, generalize to others, and finally, suggest alternatives or solutions to the problem.

For example, a teacher questions students about a picture of unemployment lines, a situation familiar to many class members. After talking about the elements of the picture and naming the problem, students talk about their own experiences. The teacher then asks, "Why do you think it is difficult to find work?" After students state their opinions, the teacher directs the discussion beyond the students' individual experiences. Do they know other people out of work who can't get jobs? Finally, the teacher encourages discussion on alternatives. How can the students get more training and/or education? What collective actions can they take? Do they understand what affirmative action is?

The inductive questioning strategy of problem-posing stresses that teaching people to think is important and applicable at all language levels. Learning to think is a step-by-step process that requires students to learn by doing. Teachers can't just communicate information; we must assume the role of asking questions of students and of expecting students to ask questions of us.

To develop thinking skills, we start at a simple descriptive level, asking students to describe people or places or events. At the descriptive level, students learn vocabulary, language structures, and become interested in the discussion content.

We then move to a projective or analytic level, asking students to say what they think, to make inferences, to generalize or to evaluate. Hilda Taba pioneered a theoretical construct of a cognitive task hierarchy for teaching students to think (Taba 1965). Her cognitive steps in many ways parallel Freire's problem-posing process. Students are asked first, for a literal description (Freire's naming the problem); second, an affective response (Freire's questions, how do people feel about the problem); third, inferences (Freire's why questions, asking for causes); fourth, generalization (Freire's social context); and finally, application and evaluation for other situations (Freire's step, what should be done). The major difference between the two thinkers is in the final step. Taba asks for summations and applications of a new perspective to other situations. Freire asks for *action* on alternatives to problems based on the new perspective.

To teach thinking skills, we must develop our own listening and questioning skills, and know how to focus and direct discussions to higher levels of thought. For example, one classroom dialogue about neighborhood problems started on a descriptive level:

"What's on your street? "There are houses on one side and there's a farm on the other side.

What do you like about your street? I like the school and the Mexicans. I can talk to them.

What don't you like?" I don't like the smelly farm. I don't like the noise. There are too many dogs."

When the teacher asked the question, "why," the students were forced to think on a higher level:

"Why are there so many dogs?	"Because there are a lot of robberies.
Why are there so many robberies?	People don't have money. They need money to eat, for clothes.
Why don't people have money?"	There's too little work."

As we see, the question "why" is critical for teaching thinking skills. "Why" questions allow people to project out of their personal experiences into a broader understanding or debate of opinions.

Projective questions, however, can be too difficult for starting discussion in ESL classes, especially for people who are not used to freely expressing opinions or who are restricted by language. Problem-posing therefore begins concretely in an English class, with teachers starting at the descriptive level to reinforce language. In the first days of class, students can learn the question words: who, what, where, why, when, and how, and exchange information from the very start. Some may need encouragement, as many normally expect the teacher to do the asking. An equal exchange between teachers and students is not possible with beginners, since students still need instruction in vocabulary and grammar. Yet the questioning strategy encourages students to draw from their own experience, curiosity, and language competence to communicate in English.

When problem-posing, the role of the teacher is not only to ask questions, but to provide any necessary information that will move the dialogue to a higher level of thinking. Teachers must be careful not to impose their worldview, but to encourage students in their own critical thinking. Likewise, teachers should be cautious about assuming leadership on solutions to local problems. People from the community become their own leaders; students from ESL classes could become these leaders or join others as they realize community issues can be tackled.

CODES

After teachers listen to the concerns of their students and select a theme or a series of problems, they draw up lessons in the form of codes to stimulate problem-posing. Codes (or "codifications" in Freire's terms) are concrete physical expressions that combine all the elements of the theme into one representation. They can take many forms: photographs, drawings, collages, stories, written dialogues, movies, songs. Codes are more than visual aids for teaching. They are at the heart of the educational process because they initiate critical thinking.

No matter what the form, a code is a projective device that is emotionally laden and identifiable to students. Discussion of the problem will liberate energy that can stimulate creativity and raise motivation for using English. A good code should have these basic characteristics:

1. It must represent a daily problem situation that is immediately recognizable to students. (They already deeply know what is being talked about.)

2. That situation, chosen because it contains personal and social affect, is presented as a problem with inherent contradictions. The code (picture, story, etc.) should illustrate as many sides of the contradiction as possible, yet be simple enough for students to project their own experience.

3. The code should focus on one problem at a time, but not in a fragmentary way. It should suggest connections to other themes in people's lives.

4. The code should not provide solutions to the problem, but should allow students to develop their own solutions from their experience.

5. The problem presented should not be overwhelming to students. There should be room for small actions that address the problem even if they don't solve it. Local community issues usually provide opportunities for students to have an impact with small-scale actions.

In essence, a code sums up or "codifies" into one statement a problem (or contradiction) that people recognize in their lives: need for English vs. loss of native culture, stress at work vs. need for work, disappointment vs. hope from expectations in the U.S. Each problem is complex without narrowly defined good and bad sides. Students can project their own feelings and opinions in an attempt to negotiate solutions.

For example, students often have difficulty not being understood and not understanding English-speakers. This problem can be codified into many situations; one possibility is a dialogue of a non-English speaker attempting to order food from a waitress who is pressured on her job. Teachers can ask students to identify the feelings of impatience and nervousness on both sides, the negative attitudes English speakers often have, and the defensiveness that causes students often to relinquish their equality. Solutions emerge when students realize the discomfort of both parties, and the necessity for them of taking risks to get respect.

After codifying the problem, teachers present the code and use the inductive questioning process to "decode" the problem in a five-step procedure.

These are the tools for dialogue.

Tools for Dialogue

1. Have students describe or name the content and feelings in the code: "*What* do you see?"

2. Ask students to define the problem concretely: "What is the problem here?" Address as many sides of the issue as possible.

3. Elicit similar problem situations in students' lives: "Do you also experience this? How is it the same? How is it different? How do you *feel* about it?" (Also ask if anyone has coped successfully with this issue before. Draw on their successes as well as their difficulties.)

4. Direct students to fit their individual experiences into a larger historical, social, or cultural perspective. Ask them to project opinions: "*Why* is there a problem? Why do you think?"

5. Encourage students to discuss alternatives and solutions: "What can you *do*?" Have students attempt small actions that will provide a new perspective on this problem or in some way ameliorate it. Again, ask for success stories.

Consider the following example of a classroom dialogue based on these questions. The teacher presented a picture of a Chinese home scene with the mother making wonton. The mother was speaking Chinese to her daughter; her daughter was answering, "No, I don't want to. I want to go play." The teacher showed this picture to explore the many aspects of the problem: why are children losing their parents' culture; what social pressures encourage them to "forget" the foreign languge; how do parents feel; how do children feel; etc.

One class pursued the following discussion from this picture code as the teacher asked them questions in the five step process.

First, the teacher asked students to describe what was happening in the picture.

TEACHER: MANY STUDENTS:

1. *What do you see?*

    "What's in the room?   "It's a kitchen. A chair. A table.
    What country are the objects
        from?   From the United States. That's
                                         from China.

    What is the mother saying?   I don't know. It's Chinese.
    What language is she speaking?   Chinese.
    What is the daughter saying?   I don't want to. I want to go
                                         play.

    What language is she speaking?"   English."

The second step addressed the conflict between mother and daughter, with parents understanding that their children need English, though wanting their children to speak Chinese.

2. *What's the problem here?*

"What is the mother doing?   "She's making wonton.
Does the daughter know how?   I don't know. Maybe. Maybe not.

Why not?   You can buy wonton in the store.
—Maybe she not help her mother.

Does the daughter speak Chinese?   Maybe, a little.
Where is the daughter from?   Not China. She's American.
—No, she's Chinese-American.

Does the mother speak English?   I don't think so.
Does the mother want her daughter to speak Chinese?"   Oh yes.
—But she needs English too."

Step three included questions applying the problem to students' lives and their feelings about the issue.

3. *Is this your problem?*

"Do your children speak your language?
          "Mine speak Spanish. They live with my father.
—My son only speaks English.

Do their friends speak your language?
          They only speak Spanish at home.
—Only one. He gets embarrassed with others.

When will your children speak your language?
at home?
How do you feel about it?
          My daughter likes to teach the baby.
—Oh, Jessie loves Spanish T.V.
          Oh, I want him to speak Chinese.
—I like them to talk Spanish.

Do your children know about your country?
Do you want them to?
Do they know how to cook your food?"
          Yes, a little. Some things.
          Oh yes.

          I don't cook too much.
—Yes, they know. They help."

Step four, asking "why" is primary to the decoding process. Often teachers only have to ask, "But why?" to move students' thinking to a higher level. The question, "Why not?" solicits students' opinions equally well.

4. *Why is there a problem?*

"How do they learn about your countries?
What about school?

"At home.
Sometimes.
—I don't know. Kim never says anything.
—Sometimes, they teach about holidays.
—I don't think they teach a lot.

Why not? Why don't schools teach about your countries?

I don't know.
—They don't think it's important.
—This is the United States.
—But children can't speak Chinese at school.

Why not?
Do teachers speak their language?

Teachers want to teach English.

Maybe. The teacher of my children speaks Spanish a little.
—My son's teacher don't speak Chinese.

Why not?
When don't your children speak your language?
Are they embarrassed?

It's too hard.

With friends. At school.
I don't know. But my son don't speak Chinese.
—Jessie too. She gets mad and doesn't talk to my father.

Why are they embarrassed?

Their friends only talk English.
—Sometimes at school other kids call my daughter bad names.

What do they say?"

Oh, I don't know. You Mexican! But she's American."

Finally, the teacher asked what students could do about the problem.

5. *What can you do?*

"Can schools teach your language?

"Yes, they teach Spanish one time a day.
—But why not more times a day?
—Why don't they teach my language?

Are there schools with bilingual programs?

I think so.
—That school is far. I want my son close to home.

What do you think about bilingual programs?

I like them.
—I want my children to speak English.
—But I want them to speak Chinese too.

Does your state have a bilingual education law? What does it say?

There are more than ten in my son's class.
—Why don't we have bilingual classes?
—I don't know. They learn at home.
—My children get embarrassed. I want them to learn Spanish at school.
—Send them to Mexico.
—I can't. They need respect here.

What classes do you want schools to have?

Classes in language.
—Yes, classes on different countries also."

What about your culture?
Can you teach the teachers about your country? your culture?"

In this dialogue, students perceived that the problem of maintaining culture and language extended beyond their personal experiences. With this understanding, they may stop blaming themselves for inadequate parenting, or they may gain the self-confidence to take action.

The decoding process creates an exciting classroom interaction. Every discussion inspired by a code will be different, depending on what issues are central to that group of students. Teachers can't and shouldn't know the answers to their questions. The inductive questions solicit students' opinions which lead to new ideas for teachers as well as for students.

In summary, the problem-posing approach has three major components:

1. LISTENING: Teachers start listening and observing before class begins and continue during and outside classroom interactions. Through their observations, teachers define and codify students' concerns for use in structured language learning and dialogue.

2. DIALOGUE: Using codes in the classroom, the dialogue approach employs decoding questions toward the goals of critical thinking and action. Teachers and students become co-learners. The dialogue approach mitigates language-learning conflict as students share their lives and culture with each other and the teacher.

3. ACTION: Dialogue is not a neutral process; it attempts to move learning from the level of information and skills to consequences and actions outside of the classroom. Action oriented problem-posing offers an opportunity for students to exercise control in class and in the rest of their lives.

To end this chapter, a chart compares problem-posing with four other major ESL approaches. Though non-inclusive, the chart graphically depicts the conceptual uniqueness of the problem-posing approach as applied to ESL teaching. The four approaches are: counseling or community language learning, situational approaches (survival and competency-based ESL), values clarification or cultural relativism, and notional/functional.

COMPARISON OF FREIRE'S PROBLEM-POSING APPROACH AND OTHER ESL METHODOLOGIES
(Moriarty and Wallerstein)

Methodology	Similarities	Differences
CL/CLL Counseling Learning/ Community Language Learning	• extends beyond the artificial environment of the classroom • attempts to use language creatively, not just repetitively • topics for discussion determined by students • emphasizes group and social interaction • demonstrates relevance of conflict and emotions to learning	• counselor/teacher doesn't ask questions, but simply translates; Freire teacher proceeds by questioning and dialogue • topics for discussion can be anything (Curran's examples—a trip to Tokyo, miniskirts); Freire content is always posed as a problem or central concern for the group • CL/CLL teacher participates as expert translator; Freire teacher participates as a peer
Survival ESL Competency-based (CBE)/(situational approaches)	• attempts to deal with adult situations • shows relevance of learning to daily life • emphasizes needs assessment and feedback for evaluation • bases pattern of competencies on social inequities	• CBE emphasizes skills to cope and assimilate; Freire emphasizes skills to create and change problem situations • Freire focuses on the survival skills and strengths that students already have • Freire emphasizes teacher and students as co-learners
Values Clarification Cultural Relativism	• affirms students' expression of feelings and value statements • encourages participation by all • teacher is nonjudgmental	• values clarification remains at individualistic level; Freire views values and cultural attitudes as a group creation
Notional/Functional	• assumes communicative competence as starting point • uses language with its social context and purpose (opinions, intentions, emotions) • teaches language that students need • organizes teaching by content and integrated skills	• life-skills are taught for individual competence; Freire emphasizes collective approach • not./funct. organizes curriculum by purpose and need only; Freire takes problem-orientation and thinking skills as major need • Freire adds cultural context to expressions and communication

Chapter 3

Teaching Techniques

Teaching English, as we all know, is more than supplying vocabulary and language structures. If we look beyond the technical difficulties in learning English skills, we find other barriers: emotional blocks, such as lack of confidence; physical barriers due to limited contact with English speakers; or social barriers, including prejudice.

Problem-posing gives people language to recognize and push against these barriers, to express opinions and feelings (similar to a notional-functional approach) and to take actions and risks in unfamiliar situations. An underlying assumption of the approach is that people develop linguistic competence through listening to language structures and through directed conversation. Listening and conversing—not drills or memorization—help students learn a new language.

The best teaching techniques thus develop comprehension skills by making people talk. And what will people talk most readily about? Themselves and the issues that affect them. Group techniques such as dialogues, pair work, and conversation circles create a supportive atmosphere where students can overcome embarrassment and gain language confidence.

Yet, as Freire suggests, "Education should never be looked at in isolation. It is not that methods and techniques are not important. But they must serve the objectives contained in the cultural plan" (Freire 1978). The teaching techniques presented in this section serve a cultural and social function: to provide students with language skills while expanding their worldviews.

An example of a grammar lesson which integrates English practice and world view appears in the AUTOBIOGRAPHY student unit. Near the beginning of any new class, I ask students, "What are you?" They reply, "I'm a student. I'm a mechanic. I'm a housewife." When I ask, "Are you a teacher?" they invariably say no. Then I ask, "What can you teach? What can you teach me?" If they have trouble answering, I suggest, "Can you teach Vietnamese? Can you teach me to cook Mexican food?" Even in a beginning class, they are able to respond, "Yes, I can," or "No, I can't." Again I ask, "Are you a teacher?" With each "no" answer, I'll ask, "Can you teach me _____?" If they're more advanced, they will be able to ask each other, "What can you teach me?" Though the exchanges are meant to practice a grammatical form, the answers have meaningful impact on students' self-images. Every "yes" answer reinforces their self-esteem and confidence. This exercise can set the classroom mood for students and teachers to approach learning as a mutual exchange.

CODES

Each unit has eight to ten codes. As discussed earlier, codes are concrete expressions of a theme or problem which carries emotional and social impact for the students.

They can be used with students at all language abilities, in single or mixed-level classes. Beginners may be able to learn only the vocabulary and respond on a descriptive level. More advanced students will be able to talk analytically about the causes of the problem.

The following code forms appear in the STUDENT UNITS: *Written Dialogues and Role-play, Stories,* and *Pictures.*

WRITTEN DIALOGUES AND ROLE-PLAYS

Written dialogues (with many parts for students to act out) encourage full participation and active discussion. They introduce the vocabulary and structures that will be used for the freer role-play stage. To begin the lesson, the teacher reads aloud the dialogue or encourages the more advanced students to take a part. Students can repeat after the teacher for intonation and pronunciation. In the first reading, the teacher clarifies all vocabulary. Then different class members (even beginners) can alternate reading the parts in front of the class. As they begin to get comfortable, students can act out the dialogue without their papers. Acting out parts generally leads to improvisations and unexpected, humorous twists to the role-plays. Props can also enliven the role-play interactions. Written dialogues and role-plays are excellent tools for raising the class' energy level, developing listening skills, and for broadening students' ability to converse in unfamiliar situations in and outside of class.

Most of the dialogues in the student units are written in three parts. Three people in front of the class keep people's attention without being confusing, and also diminish a cultural prohibition that might arise out of a man and a woman talking to each other.

The dialogues can also be simplified to individual, pair, or group exercises the day after a role-play for reinforcement of vocabulary and grammar.

STORIES

The stories in the student units are examples of codes which teachers can produce after listening to their students. The best stories come directly from students. As students tell about their lives during discussions, teachers can take notes and rewrite these stories for the next day's lesson. By transcribing these discussions or writing down students' stories, teachers are demonstrating the importance of students' thoughts and the fact that everybody is a teacher. If the subject is too personal or the teacher wants to address a more general problem, the stories can be fictionalized. (Teachers should always ask permission to use students' names and stories, thereby preventing any embarrassment.)

More advanced students can write down their own stories for the class to use the next day. If they have trouble with writing, teachers can ask concrete questions that help students order their stories. Many students do not have writing skills comparable to their speaking abilities. They can dictate their stories to the teacher or to more advanced students. Dictating or writing their own stories will reinforce reading and vocabulary skills and enhance students' belief in their own worth.

Other stories and reading matter can come from newspaper articles, school bulletins, community leaflets, or signs. They can also come from phone books, welfare or food stamp forms, advertisements, letters from their children's teachers, or from conversations in which students fantasize about their goals and ideals.

When writing stories as codes, keep in mind certain guidelines. Focus on a problem, but let it unfold by the characters' telling of the story. Leave the problem unresolved for students to come to their own conclusions. Make it emotionally involving to ensure a strong student reaction. Keep it relatively brief—50–200 words with the proper mix of vocabulary, language level, and grammar.

Students can read the stories out loud, discuss the issues, write answers to comprehension questions, and write about their own experiences in similar situations. The result is a class which continually develops its own curriculum.

PICTURES (SLIDES, PHOTOGRAPHS, DRAWINGS, COLLAGES, PHOTO-STORIES, STRIP-STORIES)

Teaching with pictures provides endless possibilities for learning vocabulary, holding discussions, creating dialogues and stories, or writing exercises. Students can respond to pictures with their own feelings and opinions, or create pictures and picture-stories to express their experiences. Like stories, pictures can be brought into the classroom by both teachers and students.

In a simple lesson, teachers will show a photo, drawing, collage, or slide and ask "What do you see?" If the picture is a face, teachers can ask, "How old is the person, where is she from, how does she feel, etc. . . ." Answers elicit new vocabulary and discussions about the picture. If the teacher has drawn a code representing an issue, questions will follow the five-step problem-posing process. It is interesting to note that teachers may have one theme or issue in mind when drawing up the code, yet students may find something quite different. Pictures allow students to select their own issues.

Photographs are easy to find. Many thrift stores sell old magazines such as *National Geographic*, which contain pictures of peoples all over the world, including countries where ESL students come from. Other magazines provide photographs of objects and everyday life in the United States. To open discussion, teachers can also take pictures of the neighborhood or of people in class. If the school or students have cameras (preferably Polaroid), they can take their own pictures of anything they like. Students may want to bring in family pictures, which would enhance the family unit by focusing the vocabulary on students' families and personal histories. An ambitious class can also produce illustrated photo-stories. Photo-novellas in comic book form are popular reading in Latin America; they lend themselves well to a class project. Students can use their own photographs to write a dialogue about family life or can take new pictures to produce the photo-novella.

Drawings by the teacher can pull together the many aspects of a problem into one code. Students can also draw their own pictures in response to questions: "What do you like or want," or in response to commands: "Draw your family, your home, or what you don't like," etc. Students can caption their drawings; this will generate further discussion and further writing exercises. Students can also plan out and draw strip-stories. Teachers can introduce the first strip-story by having students illustrate sentences within an action sequence. The drawings in the sentences can then be mixed up for students to reorder in front of the classroom. Students can write their own action stories for others to illustrate and practice with.

Collages allow students to use magazine photographs and other materials in creative ways. Teachers can bring in examples of collages on a theme, such as faces, styles of work, clothes of many countries. Tasks with collages can start out simply: find pictures of things you like/hate, that you have/don't have. Students can write a sentence to complement each picture. They can also make a collage about themselves, about their family, about their home country. Each collage can, of course, generate discussions. The action of making the collage in class increases the energy level and group interaction, and teaches functional vocabulary—pass the scissors, hand me the paste, etc.

PUPPETS

Puppets are marvelous motivational tools for increasing participation and multicultural awareness (Condon). Puppets, in the broadest sense, are any moveable object that students can make speak or come alive—a hand, spoon, a shoe, a picture. They provide security for people who may be too shy or embarrassed to speak when others focus on their faces. They can be used with students of all ages and abilities. Photographs of people stuck on the ends of pencils can talk to each other in strict dialogues or free-flow conversation.

More elaborate puppets can be made from cardboard figures and have movable parts that can be attached with pipe cleaners, strings, or clips.

Puppet people can become marionettes or "flexiflans" which are figures placed on a flannel board and moved around as they tell a story (Crone and Hunter 1980). Story props can also be cut out of cardboard and situated on the flannel board.

Puppets can act out problem-posing codes. Teachers or students can re-enact folk tales, stories from students' cultures, or dialogues that may be too threatening if students talked face to face. Newspaper stories of highly charged community concerns can be acted out to discharge emotions before discussing solutions.

TOOLS FOR DIALOGUE

After every code in the Student Units, the Tools for Dialogue section takes teachers and students through the five problem-posing steps: 1) Describe *what* you see; 2) Define the problem; 3) Apply the problem to your lives: tell *how* you feel about it; 4) Discuss the social/economic reasons: tell *why* there is a problem; 5) Ask *what* you can do about it.

Questions in each of these stages will take students through an analysis of the theme or issue in the code. These questions are only suggestions; teachers may want to pose different ones or omit those not relevant for that particular class.

The descriptive questions of steps one, two, and three are more straight-forward and easier to answer. Yet the projective questions, steps four and five—asking for opinions, explanations, speculations—challenge us as teachers and students. We can ask students, "Why is this happening? What do you think? Can you guess?" Sometimes it helps to start on a simpler level with the word "maybe." Talking about a picture, teachers can start with, "I don't know what she's feeling, but *maybe* she's sad. I think she's sick. What do you think?" Since it's clear there is no "right" or "wrong" answer, students will respond more readily, "I don't know. *Maybe*, she's _____." Step five encourages students to think of small or large actions they can take. These will range from students making observations in the community or home about the problem raised in the code, to obtaining outside information from a community service or organizing a meeting about the problem. Even small observation homework actions give students confidence and increase the connection students feel between the classroom and their lives.

The teacher may decide to incorporate a few of the questions in reading and writing exercises after students have discussed the questions orally.

PRACTICE

Each written code in the student units emphasizes communicative skills and structures. Brief structural drills are highlighted in the *Practice*. This section can be done before, after, or during the decoding discussion. The Practice Section is not a definitive one; other structures might be raised in the codes.

While grammar must be taught systematically, exercises should be integrated, whenever possible, into problem-posing discussions. After role-playing a trip to the grocery store, for example, teachers can activate to the present tense, "Where do you shop; where does she shop; where do they shop?" The answers provide a reality-based grammar lesson: "I shop at Lucky's; she shops at Star Market; they shop at Stop and Shop." A discussion can follow on how shopping at these places is different.

This exercise would not substitute for lessons on the present tense, but drills like this can be helpful for short periods. Providing a context for grammar allows teachers to develop different techniques for teaching it; either with the group, in pairs (particularly for review), or with individual writing exercises.

CONVERSATION CIRCLES

A conversation circle can also be useful in the middle of the Tools for Dialogue discussion. When teachers ask how a situation applies to their students, they may find that everyone has something to share. Breaking up the class into small conversation circles gives everyone a chance to ask/answer the questions again. If the situation is meaningful, people will genuinely want to hear the answers. After the full discussion, teachers may want to follow up the conversation circle with pairwork during which students "interview" one another and write down what they find out.

READING COMPREHENSION SKILLS

As the written codes are read aloud, teachers can focus on students' reading comprehension and vocabulary skills before or during the decoding discussion. A brainstorming activity could result in writing words or ideas on the board that come from the code. Students can develop categories from the brainstorming, reorder the ideas in their original sequence, and pick out the main idea from the ones on the board. Students can dictate sentences to the teacher which can become simple cloze or multiple choice exercises.

WRITING EXERCISES

Although the Student Units primarily stress speaking and reading skills, learning to write is equally important. As mentioned earlier, teachers can develop writing exercises directly from the Tools for Dialogue questions or from the suggested grammar practice. In-class writing or homework assignments can reinforce the dialogue vocabulary and allow for more in-depth exploration of the subject. Students can also write stories similar to codes presented in this book.

Many students may be illiterate, even though they have some speaking ability in English. Often no special literacy classes will be available for them. These students should be encouraged to participate in the dialogues and role-play through listening closely. This book does not attempt to present special methods for literacy students, except to emphasize that problem-posing about issues in people's lives applies to every language level.

SUGGESTED ACTIVITIES (ACTIONS)

After each code (dialogue, story, picture) the Suggested Activities section offers additional ways to pursue the topic or engage in further language learning. These activities often propose the actions students could take to gain a new perspective on, or solve the problem. They include observations in and out of class, role-plays with alternative endings, outside speakers, and field trips. Because this is primarily a teacher resource book, many of the suggested activities are not fully developed. Each teacher will be able to expand on what is presented.

ACTIVE TECHNIQUES

Active techniques are based on the premise that body movements, gestures and rhythms help students relax. The learning by doing places the new language more easily in students' long-term memory. In general, they break up a time of sitting, get circulation moving, and raise people's energy especially after a day's work. These techniques include ones mentioned earlier, having students act out dialogues, draw pictures, manipulate puppets, or develop a strip story.

Active techniques also include simple methods which work particularly well with beginners—flash cards, total physical response (Asher), live action English (Romijn and Seely 1980), jazz chants (Graham 1978), or singing songs.

Games like *Simon Says* are fun and appealing. Students can invent a machine and act out movements as they say what they are doing. They can pair up and play communication games, like *Battleship* or give map directions for a hidden board (Winn-Bell Olsen 1977). They can play charades or mime simple actions for other students to guess. If teachers feel comfortable about using these techniques, students may let go of their embarrassment and join in.

Active techniques can also integrate problem-posing. Many times the technique itself acts as a code for students to discuss: role-plays are both active and very effective for generating discussions. Other times, active techniques start with vocabulary and lead into a code. Making videos of the actions or role-plays allow for more problem-posing. Students can reflect on the feelings behind the dialogues and analyze the non-verbal body language to see whether it communicated different attitudes than they wanted. Long-term projects (writing plays or radio scripts) can also include problem-posing within their content and dialogue.

BEGINNERS

The dialogue and problem-posing method works best for students with limited speaking ability, or for those who have lived in the U.S. for a long time, but do not consider themselves English speakers. Both these groups are accustomed to the sound of English, even if they can't speak it. They hear English on television. Their children often speak it. Conversations surround them, so they gain a receptive competence in English; they understand more than they speak. Through the dialogue approach, students have the opportunity to pull together what they already know into a coherent form.

For beginners, dialogue can be difficult, but critical thinking is no less important for them than more proficient speakers. People who don't speak English are often the *most* isolated from Anglo society. As much as anyone, they require a curriculum reflecting how they live and what they need to survive. Although a beginning-level class cannot go through all the problem-posing steps, they can answer questions in the first three steps: "What do you see; what's the problem; and how does this apply to you?" If the teacher can kindle a group interest in each other's lives and cultures, it will later translate into dialogue as students learn more English.

PROBLEM-POSING TECHNIQUES FOR BEGINNERS

1. Begin with the question words: who, what, where, when, why, how. These are tools which make students active rather than passive participants in the class. They will be able to question the teacher and initiate their own discussions. Technically it is best to introduce the words separately. They sound similar in English and can be easily confused.

2. Begin with simple autobiographies using the most common and important questions for survival: "Where do you live; where do you work; where do you come from?" The teacher can write the students' responses into a story for class the next day.

3. Use flashcards to introduce vocabulary, bits of sentence structure, even students' names. Literacy students especially benefit from this sight/sound learning and from manipulating the objects in their hands as they speak the words. In addition, the room can be decorated with the flashcards next to pictures or organized by subject.

   Use street or building signs to develop survival vocabulary and sight recognition words. Signs demonstrate that students already know words, and strengthen the connection between the class and the community.

4. Experiment with Total Physical Response or Live Action English, with teacher and students giving each other commands. With these methods students learn by seeing the actions, hearing the words, doing the actions, and commanding other students. Actions can also extend to situations which could become codes. After students describe their work, "I sort the tomatoes, I throw the bad ones away, I leave the good ones on the belt, I put them in a box, I lift the box, etc.," they can have a discussion about the nature of their work.

5. From the beginning introduce words to express emotions: "I feel happy today; I'm embarrassed; I'm sad; I'm homesick; I was tired all day."

6. Use the "Microwave" method to teach a dialogue. This method focuses on only one grammar structure at a time. (Harding and Delisle 1968) Puppets can help teach these dialogues.

school teacher	I'm a school teacher. (use of I'm)
farm worker	I'm a farm worker . . .
bus driver	He's a bus driver. (use of He's)
storekeeper	She's a storekeeper . . .
What do you do?	I'm a truck driver.
What does your wife do?	She's a (schoolteacher).

7. Teach pronunciation in small segments. Pronunciation is important because of the difference in sound systems between English and other languages. Pronunciation lessons, however, should not necessarily be aimed at wiping out a "foreign accent" which is a valid part of people's culture in the U.S. Teachers must be careful also not to interrupt and inhibit students' conversation by injecting pronunciation corrections.

TEAM/PEER TEACHING

Teaching is difficult when students have different language and literacy proficiency levels. Even among beginners there will be differences. The best solution for the different ability levels seems to be team teaching. The class can be separated into different groups for half the class time, with teachers giving different exercises, directions on overheads, or cassette recorder lessons, and dividing their time between groups. Despite different levels, the class can come back together for structured dialogues and role-plays; everyone will enjoy the drama. Less advanced students will usually understand the dialogue though they might be less able to act it out.

If team teaching is not possible, the teacher can get help from more advanced students. The class can be divided into groups of three or four people at mixed levels or at the same level. In the mixed level groups, the more advanced students can teach beginners if the teacher provides a carefully structured lesson for a conversation circle. Alternately, groups of similar proficiency levels enable teachers to devote extra attention to beginners while the intermediates pursue writing and reading assignments or independent discussions. Structured pair practice is also good for grammar review and for encouraging students to work independently.

✓FOREIGN LANGUAGE IN THE CLASSROOM

Whether students should be allowed to speak their native language in the classroom is the subject of much controversy. In multicultural classrooms, where students speak languages unknown to their teachers, multilingual lessons are nearly impossible.

In many situations, the native language facilitates students' learning of English. The question becomes when and how to allow its usage. Allowing students to translate and explain meanings to each other can create a supportive, non-stressful atmosphere. Literacy students especially need this support. Through their native language, students can help each other catch up after absences. Native languages can add humor to the class as students joke or comment to one another and then attempt to translate what they've said into English. Most importantly, students can begin to learn about each other's culture as they hear the different languages. To witness students asking each other about their native language or about their culture is always impressive and exhilarating.

When teachers work predominantly with a single language group—especially in an area where English is not the primary language—teachers obviously communicate more effectively if they know the students' language. Bilingual teaching then becomes an option, and the students' language can be used for explanations or for important discussions they still can't manage totally in English. To promote English learning during these discussions, teachers can jot down phrases on the board and translate them into English as the discussion proceeds. Follow-up lessons focusing on related English vocabulary will have special meaning from a discussion like this. Teachers with bilingual abilities also affirm the validity of bicultural/bilingual communities in the United States.

BILINGUAL LITERACY

One bilingual literacy method enables students to begin writing "English" without knowing how to spell. Speakers of Spanish (and other phonetic languages) often have difficulty writing, spelling, and even pronouncing English. Teachers therefore may often wonder what students are trying to say or write. Many times students want to know the meaning of an English expression, but teachers can't understand them enough to respond.

One Illinois teacher, Tomas Kalmar, began to solve this problem by asking his Spanish-speaking students to write down the expressions they heard—*as* they heard them. Students responded, writing in Spanish phonetics: "Urrillap." and "Juaruyusei?" Another student wanted to know: "Limisi." And another: "Jamach?" These expressions translated into the English: 1) "Hurry up." 2) "How do you say?" 3) "Let me see." and 4) "How much?" Though the correct English spelling was very different, spelling the words in "eye dialect" made them accessible. This technique excited students to learn as they eagerly compiled a daily dictionary of phrases they wanted to know.

Although the underlying linguistic assumptions for this new method are not clear yet, teachers can experiment with its effectiveness in their own classrooms. This method works from two different angles.

In the first approach, students write down the English expressions they have heard (as they've heard them) in a column in the middle of the board. Then the teacher determines the meaning of the eye dialect (or phonetic spelling) and writes the correct English words in a left-hand column and the Spanish translations on the right. The second angle is for students to start from the Spanish words they want to learn. After they write the Spanish, the teacher tells them the English and asks them to write the words as they phonetically hear the sounds. The teacher will then transpose the words into correct English spelling.

If this technique is incorporated into every class period for a short time, different students can record the three-column list for the whole class. The teacher can xerox and hand back the list to all students for a class dictionary.

One class wrote these phrases: (Read the middle column first.)

I need	ai nid	necesito
truth	chrud	la verdad
where's he from?	uers ji from?	de donde viene el?
how old are you?	ja oldayu?	cuantos años tienes?
I'll be back.	avivac	ahorita regreso

With this method, the words that students learn are not memorized nonsensical sounds from a text or a teacher. Instead, the learning begins and ends with students' naming the words they want to know and the reality they want to understand.

Chapter 4
Techniques to Be Avoided

Techniques which inhibit learning by causing embarrassment or boredom should clearly be avoided in the classroom. A lively atmosphere is essential for teaching adults; other priorities can cause them to drop out anytime. Students need variety: active techniques, reading/writing exercises, direct instruction, group interaction, etc. Within each daily period, I have found that presenting and decoding the code works well for an hour, followed by a half-hour for grammar or writing exercises related to the code. (Teachers with shorter classes can adjust the breakdown according to what works best for each group.) Students are more likely to maintain a high level of involvement when they talk directly to each other about real issues and concerns in their daily lives.

One caution about using student experiences in discussions: be careful not to ask for information which embarrasses students or puts their legal or work status in jeopardy. Some students may need to withhold certain personal experiences, such as having illegal immigrant status. Present stories about fictionalized people or real people not known to the class. You can still hold discussions of sensitive but important issues, and grant students the choice to volunteer their experiences. Discussion of sensitive issues can be extremely beneficial to students, but it must be done with discretion and respect.

SITUATIONAL METHOD

One teaching technique often used is the Situational Method. This method has potential for building competency and for discussion, but I believe it has been much abused. The Situational Method uses dialogues that contain the survival vocabulary people need in their daily lives, i.e. calling repair people, working in different jobs, going to the welfare office, and handling emergencies.

Yet the content of situational dialogues often deserves criticism for being unrealistic or patronizing. The situations employed in many dialogues do not accurately describe the economic and cultural realities of non-English speaking working class people in the United States.

Here is a dialogue from one situational method book.

At the Doctor's Office

Mrs. Garcia: Is Doctor Smith in?

Nurse: What is your name? Do you have an appointment?

Mrs. Garcia: No, but I'm very sick. My name is Mrs. Garcia. My friend told me to see Dr. Smith.

Nurse: Let me speak to the doctor. (returning to the reception room) Dr. Smith will see you after the next patient.

Dr. Smith: What is your trouble, Mrs. Garcia?

Mrs. Garcia: I have a bad pain in my chest. I cough all the time.

Dr. Smith: Your lungs seem clear. I'll give you a prescription. Have it filled at the drug store. Try to keep quiet and get some rest.

This dialogue contains a number of incorrect assumptions. The first is that poor, working class or unemployed people have their own doctors. In reality, these people (who comprise many ESL classes) go to clinics, don't have the same doctors each time, and have to wait in line, even with appointments. Second, the doctor's advice demonstrates a misunderstanding of the patient's economic status. Working class people do not usually have the leisure to rest from their jobs, especially if they are non-unionized. Furthermore, their work conditions often create or exacerbate their medical problems. Even if they take time off, they encounter the same problems as soon as they go back to work.

The dialogue is also superficial. It doesn't confront any of the feelings or conflicts people may have when going to the doctor. They may have trouble explaining their illness with their limited English, feel humiliated, or believe they are not receiving the proper care. Women may wait all afternoon without being seen. They then face having to miss more work, or pay for more childcare or transportation. Many cannot afford the medicines and the fees. Dialogues which reflected the students' lives, on the other hand, would generate much discussion on the adequacy of health care in this country.

Some dialogues, as illustrated below, also contain stereotypic characters or situations.

The Car Wash Worker

Manager: Good morning, my name is Ben Brown. I'm the manager.

José: Good morning, Mr. Brown. I'm the new boy. My name is José.

Mr. Brown: Glad to meet you, José. I'll show you around the plant before we open up.

José: You have a big place. Do you have a lot of rich customers?

Mr. Brown: I don't know how rich they are, but some of them drive expensive cars. They expect good work.

José: I like to drive big cars.

Mr. Brown: Well, you won't start on that job. Give the cars a good cleaning. Don't miss any spots.

José: I'll do my best.

The Anglo manager is *Mr.* Brown; the worker is José, a boy. The worker is portrayed as childlike, needing to be told how to do simple work. At best, the dialogue is ambiguous as to whether José is actually a child.

And again, the dialogue is superficial. There is no exploration of feelings about work or of hierarchies on the job. I feel, however, that we have the responsibility to bring out people's feelings about their lives, their work, or the discrimination they face.

The following example contains issues that confront many students. It demonstrates a non-alienating use of the Situational Method and contains opportunities for problem-posing.

At the Clinic

Woman enters clinic, room is full of people. She walks to the desk.

Mrs. Lorca: Good morning. I want a checkup. I have a backache.

Receptionist: Have you been here before? We have forms you need to fill out.

Mrs. Lorca: Can you speak more slowly? I don't understand English very well.

Receptionist: Never mind. I'll check the records. (she checks) No, we don't have your record. Have a seat and fill out this form. Be sure to include your phone number. Do you have Med-i-cal?

Mrs. Lorca: Yes, but I forgot my card.

Receptionist: I'm sorry, you'll have to come back with your card.

Mrs. Lorca: But I work tomorrow.

Receptionist: I'm sorry. You have to bring your card. We're open from 8 to 6.

Problem-posing follows the five-step procedure:

1. Ask informational questions: "Where is Mrs. Lorca; what is wrong with her; how does she pay for the doctor?"

2. Ask questions to unfold the problems that Mrs. Lorca encounters: "What language does she speak; what language does the receptionist speak; how does she pay; why does she have to wait till tomorrow; can she return tomorrow?"

3. Apply the contradictions to students' lives. Here, there are at least three: problems of language, payment, and availability of health care. The teacher should listen for which one interests the students most. If students express greatest interest in the problem of payment, ask: "How do you pay; what happens when you forget your medical insurance card; were you treated without a card?"

4. Draw together the individual student experiences to examine the health care system: "What are the problems with state medical insurance; what is good about it; who uses the state insurance; why is there a two-tiered system?"

5. Ask students what ideas they would propose for a different system: "How would you change the payment system; what can your local clinic do?"

Whatever techniques or material we use with adults, we must take care to include issues that have importance and relevance to the students' lives.

PART TWO

Using the Student Units

This section translates the problem-posing method and teaching techniques into eight curriculum units which may serve as examples for teachers interested in the approach. The units are presented in a manner that will allow teachers to adapt or expand the materials for their own classroom needs.

The units cover eight basic themes: AUTOBIOGRAPHY, FAMILY, CULTURE AND CONFLICT, NEIGHBORHOOD, IMMIGRATION, HEALTH, WORK, and MONEY. These themes are common to most students, yet broad enough to be adapted to issues within individual classrooms. The Student Units start at a beginning level and rapidly progress to advanced beginning/intermediate in grammar, vocabulary and language structures. Teachers can begin with the issues in the dialogues and modify them to the level(s) of their own students.

Each unit contains eight *Codes* in the form of written dialogues, stories, and pictures, followed by *Tools for Dialogue* (the decoding questions), *Practice* (grammar and function exercises), *Conversation Circles* (circle pattern practice), *Writing Exercises* (in some lessons), and *Suggested Activities*. An introduction to each unit discusses the relevance of the theme and content of the eight codes which are then keyed to student interests, emotions, and needed language skills.

The first code in every unit is not usually a problem in itself; it lays a groundwork in vocabulary and descriptive skills so students can discuss the issues/problems raised in the other seven codes. In the same way, much of the first unit, AUTOBIOGRAPHY, offers a foundation for the rest of the units by providing students with communication skills to ask questions, express desires and emotions, state opinions, and talk about their lives.

A typical classroom might proceed as follows with each of the lessons:

1. Before class, teachers can select from various methods to distribute the Code to students: xeroxing the page, retyping the Code double-spaced onto a ditto master, writing it on the board, or using an overhead projector.

2. a) If the Code is a written dialogue, teachers with the more advanced students will read the dialogue aloud. During the first or second reading, teachers will clarify vocabulary and ask students to repeat lines following the teacher's pronunciation. Class members will then take turns reading the parts in front of the class. After students become comfortable, teachers can ask students to act out the dialogue without reading. The role-play generally leads to improvisation and new situations using the vocabulary. Role-plays can be done with or without props.

   b) If the Code is a story, teachers and students will read it aloud, clarifying vocabulary and pronunciation.

   c) If the Code is a picture, teachers will have to xerox the page or project it with an opaque projector.

3. After students read, role-play or look at the Code, teachers may turn to the Practice section to review particular grammatical points that emerge in the Code. Teachers can also select other features for drills or practice as appropriate for their class.

4. Then teachers begin decoding the written dialogue, story, or picture by asking the problem-posing questions listed under Tools for Dialogue. Teachers may choose to ask all of the ones listed or select those that seem appropriate. Of course, during any dialogue other questions by teachers or students will arise. With pictures, teachers may want to ask more descriptive questions (step one) to elicit more vocabulary and sentence structure. After the discussion, students may want to role-play a written dialogue again with the endings aimed at solutions to the problem.

5. At this point, teachers can choose several directions. They can proceed with the Conversation Circles and Writing Exercises, if they are provided. Conversation Circles can also be incorporated into the discussion if teachers want to emphasize certain language structures or content areas. If Writing Exercises are not provided, teachers can select five to ten questions under Tools for Dialogue to make up a writing activity that would reinforce vocabulary and grammar. These questions can be typed on a separate ditto for class- or homework.

6. Finally, teachers can choose from the Suggested Activities section which proposes a list of activities for teachers who want to develop further lessons on the same theme. The list may include suggested role-plays, active techniques, written or oral exercises, or field trips to provide links to the community.

The entire problem-posing process (discussing and practicing language from the Codes) can take from one to one and a half hours. Additional written activities or other exercises from the Suggested Activities section may extend the lesson for a longer time. This process can be easily used for half a period with the other half devoted to different teaching methods or grammar exercises.

These units can also be used in basic education and G.E.D. classes to promote dialogue. ABE students face many of the same issues as ESL students: they can of course benefit from learning to think critically. ABE teachers can expand the units to include more reading and writing skills.

WRITING A NEW CURRICULUM

With the sample units as a beginning, teachers can create new codes and lessons. Teachers will soon discover ideas for other codes within the suggested activities, and most importantly, within the discussions that arise in class after using one of the codes in this book. The beauty of using codes is that students can project their own experience and answer questions for themselves. Each class will have different interpretations of the issues and require different follow-up and new codes.

Where do we start if we're designing a curriculum unique to our own classrooms? The first step is to determine appropriate themes and sub-themes. In the first days of class, autobiographical questions elicit a picture of students' lives. At the start, we often choose lessons arbitrarily—should the class start with family issues or health problems? Yet, once we begin listening for responses, we are on the path to identifying the key concerns.

Some guidelines may make it easier to decide which problems should be included in a curriculum: Is this a situation or problem familiar to many students? Will it evoke a strong and emotional response? Is it more than a personal issue, opening up a social context? Is it rooted in students' past, present, and future conflicts and hopes? Is action possible—even small steps—or is it too overwhelming for students? If we answer yes, then the problem may be appropriate.

After deciding on a theme and a series of problems within that theme, the second step is to ask how this can be shown to students. How can I make codes? Again, using guidelines will help direct the process: focus on one problem at a time, showing the many sides to this problem. Don't offer a solution in each code; the stories or written dialogues should be left open for students to imagine solutions or strategies in their own lives.

The third step is to define what questions to ask in order to decode the problem. These will follow the five-step problem-posing process outlined in the TEACHING APPROACH, though sometimes planned questions emerge differently (or in a different order) when students are engaged in the dialogue.

Finally, we evaluate by listening to students' reactions to the code and to the decoding discussion. Where did they laugh? What generated the most interest? What helped them learn English? We must also evaluate what did *not* work and how the code could be better adapted for the next class. In other words, we continue listening to help create more curriculum. Once the class is in session, students will be able to develop their own codes through writing stories, making collages, or cooperating on group projects.

Problem-posing is an exciting approach for both teachers and students. The curriculum never stagnates; it unfolds constantly as new interests or conflicts emerge from previous dialogues. The best codes are therefore always unique to different classes. The following student units should prove fruitful for understanding students' concerns and inspiring teachers' creativity to make new codes.

I. AUTOBIOGRAPHY OVERVIEW

Language in Autobiography unit presented in following lesson plans, codes 1–8:

Vocabulary: question words—
               what (1,2)
               where (1,3)
               who (3)
               how (4)
               when (8)
               why (throughout)

               introductions (1)
               family (3)
               emotions (4)
               self-description (5)
               education (7,8)

Language functions and structures:
               express agreement (1) — I think so.
               request help (2) — Can you help me? I need _____ .
               request clarification (2) — Excuse me. I don't understand.
                                 (4) — What do you mean? What's the
                                 matter?
               express desire (7) — I want.
               express ability (8) — I can.
               use present and present progressive tenses (throughout)

An autobiographical thread is woven through all the curriculum units. Students' concerns, their families, their daily activities at home and at work, their cultural traditions, and their feelings about life in the U.S. provide the core for each unit.

The goals of this first are to establish a comfortable learning/teaching environment, to introduce students to one another, and to create a basis for people to question themselves and each other about their lives. From the beginning, written dialogues incorporate the feelings of being new to a class and new to a country, while directly addressing the conflicts and desires people have in learning English. As class members share opinions and experiences, they become comfortable and less fearful of trying out their English.

To promote this exchange, dialogues and exercises in this unit give people words to express emotions and ask questions. The first class meetings contain the basic question words: "What is your name? Where do you live? How old are you? Who do you live with? Why are you sad or happy? When do you need English?" Conversation circles build in active participation, as students question each other instead of waiting for teacher-directed questions. Even with beginning students, a first exercise such as, "What is your name?" can be used with a conversation circle. This method creates a group identity and emphasizes immediate English success with only a minimal mastery of the language.

Answers to these self-descriptive questions give teachers an understanding of the primary themes and concerns in students' lives. The specific question, "Why do you need English?" provides students with the opportunity to state the vocabulary they need and to point out situations they worry about. From these early discussions, teachers can decide which thematic unit would best follow AUTOBIOGRAPHY. Other themes will emerge from initial discussions, and then the class can move on to another unit. The units need not be taken in the same order. In addition, the simple descriptive questions will provide teachers with an informal evaluation of their students' communicative competence. How much do they understand and how easily can they produce answers? At what levels? The class period can then be divided into times for intensive small group work and for whole class interaction with dialogues and picture codes.

Written exercises come directly out of these autobiographical discussions. Intermediate students can write their own autobiographies, while beginners dictate theirs to the teacher. These written stories can be used for the following day's lesson. Students can also practice filling out forms using their personal information: employment and social services applications, school enrollment forms, alien registration cards, etc. If possible, real forms should be brought in for practice.

This unit ends with an in-depth look at the meaning of education in students' lives: what do they study now, and what do they want to study later? What do they do now and what do they want to do later? A picture code, students sitting in a circle with the teacher, generates discussions on how students learn most effectively: what they learn from teachers and what they learn from each other.

1. I'm New Here

José: Hello, my name is José Muñoz. I'm new here.
Luisa: Hello, José. I'm Luisa. This is Kim.
Kim: Glad to meet you.
José: Are you students?
Luisa: Yes, we're learning English.
José: It's hard to learn English.
Kim: I think so. How long have you been here?
José: Two months. I'm from Peru. Where are you from?
Kim: I'm from Vietnam.
José: And you?
Luisa: I'm from Arizona.

Tools for Dialogue

1. Is José new?
   What are Luisa and Kim learning?
   What languages do they speak?
   How long has José been here?

2. Is it hard to learn English?
   Where is Kim from?
   Where is Luisa from?
   Why is Luisa learning English?
   Do Spanish-speaking people live in Arizona?

3. Are you new here?
   What are you learning?
   Where are you from?
   Is it hard for you to learn English?

4. Why are you learning English?
   Is Luisa American?
   Why doesn't she speak English?
   Are there other Americans who don't speak English? Who? What do they speak?

Conversation Circle—Introductions

What's your name? What's your first name? What's your last name?
        your address?
        your phone number?
        your zip code?

Where are you from?
       do you live?

Practice

	are you learning?	I'm	
	is she	She's	
What	is he	He's	learning . . .
	are they	They're	
	are we	We're	

	learn English?
	learn Spanish?
Is it hard to	learn Vietnamese?
	drive a car . . . ?

Yes, it's hard to . . .
Yes, I think so.
No, it's not hard. It's easy.

Are you new here?
How long have you been here?
I've been here for _____ years/months.

Suggested Activities

1. Have students interview each other and introduce their partners to the class.
2. On the first day of class, make personal name cards and country name cards for the class. Mix them up and have the class tell you which cards go with which person. Use a dialogue to encourage them to remember each other's names, i.e., This is Luisa. She's from Arizona. She's been here two years.
3. Have students write their names in their own languages, and their names in English. This is an especially good activity for students whose native languages do not share the roman alphabet. Other cultures may also order family and first names in a different way from English.

2. I Need Help

Marcos: Hello, I'm new here. Can you help me?
  Chila: Sure, what do you need?
Marcos: I need an English class.
  Ofelia: Oh, I study English. Do you need classes in the day or at night?
Marcos: Excuse me. I don't understand.
  Chila: (slowly) Can you come to school in the morning or at night?
Marcos: Oh, at night.
  Ofelia: There are night classes.
Marcos: I need to learn more about auto mechanics, too.
  Chila: You should go see a counselor.
Marcos: A what?
  Chila: A counselor. Come with me. I'll help you.

Tools for Dialogue

1. What does Marcos need?
   Does he need night classes or day classes?
   What does he also want to learn?
   Where should he go for help?

2. Does he understand Ofelia?
   What does he say?
   How does he ask for help?
   Who helps him?
   What's a counselor?

3. What are you learning now?
   What do you need to learn?
   What do you need to learn in your life?
   How do you feel when you don't understand?
   Do you ask for help? Do you talk to a friend?

4. Why do you need help?
   Is it okay to ask for help?

5. Who helps you here?
   Who do you help?
   Do you know someone who is new here?
   How can you help them?

Practice

What do you need?

I need	an English class. a night class. help. a car. a boyfriend.
I need	to learn English. to eat dinner. to see a counselor. to come at night.

Suggested Activities

1. Have students role-play different mini-situations:
   Can you help me? I need an English class.
   I need a typing class.
   I need to buy eggs. Where's the store?
   I need to mail letters. Where's the mailbox?
   I need to find a job. Where's the paper?
   I need to learn English. Where's the school?

2. Have students role-play situations in which they don't understand something. They can practice:
   Excuse me. I don't understand.
   Wait a minute. I don't understand. Can you repeat that, please?
   I'm sorry. I don't understand. Please speak slowly.

3. My Family

My name is Susana. I am married to Juan. I was born in Mexico. Juan is from Costa Rica. We have two children. They were born in the United States. They are U.S. citizens. We speak Spanish at home. The children speak English at school. I'm also learning English at school. I'm happy to speak Spanish and English. I'm sad when the children only speak English. I want them to speak Spanish too.

Tools for Dialogue

1. Where was Susana born? Where was Juan born?
   How many children do they have?
   Where were the children born?
   Are the children U.S. citizens?

2. What language do they speak at home?
   What language do the children speak at school?
   When is Susana happy?
   When is she sad?

3. Where were you born?
   Are you married? Single? Divorced? Widowed?
   Do you have children?
   Where were the children born?
   What language do you speak at home?
   What language do the children speak?
   Do you want them to speak your language?

4. Why is Susana sad when the children only speak English?
   Why is it hard to speak two languages in the United States?

5. Do you think it's important for your children to speak your language?
   How can you teach your children?

Conversation Circle—My Family

Who	do you live with?
	lives in the United States?
	lives in your home country?

Where	does your mother live? your father?
	do your sisters and brothers live?

Practice

Where   were you born?
         was she born?

I was born in
She/He was born in
You were born in   _____ .
They were born in
We were born in

Writing Exercise

Have students fill in information about themselves.

My name is _____ . *My* address is _____ .

_____ phone number is _____ . I live with *my* _____

_____ (brother, sister, mother, father, children, wife . . .)

_____ family is _____ (large/small). _____ first

language is _____ . I was born in _____ .

Suggested Activity

Have students use the questions from the Conversation Circle to interview one another. Then have them complete the paragraph with the information they got during the interview. Check on pronoun usage (*my* to *his/her*; *I* to *he/she*).

4. How Do You Feel?

Practice Questions

1. How does the girl feel?
   Is she happy? Why?

2. Is she laughing?
   Is she smiling?

3. Are you happy now?
   Why? Why not?

4. What things make you happy?

5. Are you smiling now?
   Are you laughing now?

6. What things make you sad?

1. How does the woman feel?
   Is she worried? Why?

2. Are you worried now?
   Why? Why not?

3. When are you worried?

4. How does the baby feel?

5. What makes you cry?

Practice

—How are you today?	Are you	happy?
		sad?
		angry?
		worried?
		tired?
		homesick?
		sick?
	Yes, I am.	/No, I'm not; I'm _____.

—How do you feel right now?   I feel   _____.

hungry.
thirsty.
sleepy.
nervous.
bored.
hot.
cold.

—How does s(he) feel?   S(he) feels   _____.
—How do they feel?   They feel   _____.

Suggested Activities

1. Have students act out mini role-plays. For example:

Miguel: How do you feel today?　　How do you feel today?
 Maria: I'm okay. How are you?　　Not so good.
Miguel: I'm happy.　　　　　　　What's the matter?
 Maria: Why?　　　　　　　　　I'm homesick for my country.
Miguel: It's a beautiful day.　　　I'm sorry.

　　How are you today?　　　　　How are you?
　　I'm worried.　　　　　　　I'm hungry. What about you?
　　What's wrong?　　　　　　I'm not hungry, but I'm thirsty.
　　I have a test today.　　　　Let's go to the cafeteria.
　　Oh, don't worry. You'll do
　　　fine.

2. Have students ask each other how they feel. Then have them ask: How does the person on your right feel? (on your left, in front of you, behind you).
3. Use pictures of faces to demonstrate feelings. Ask: How do you think he or she feels? Why?
4. Use expressions and gestures to illustrate emotions and teach vocabulary.

5. What Does She or He Look Like?

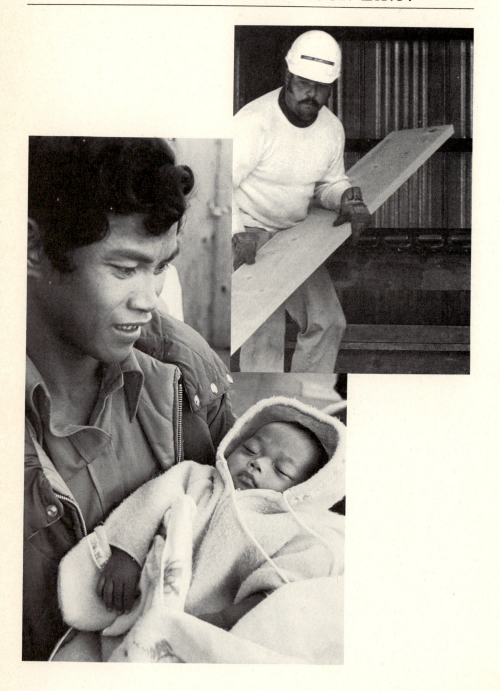

Describe the pictures:

Where is she/he from?
How old is she/he?
Is she/he young or old?
Is she/he tall or short?
    fat or thin?
    hardworking or lazy?
    pretty/handsome/ugly?
    strong or weak?
What color is her/his hair?
Is it curly or straight?
What color are her/his eyes?

What are they wearing?
They are wearing pants
        shirt
        shoes
        dress
        hat
        hard hat
        work
            clothes . . .
What are they doing?
How do they feel?

Suggested Activities

1. Use pictures like the samples to describe people orally: what they look like, how they feel, and what they are doing. Have students write or dictate descriptions.

2. Develop exercises on present progressive tense. What are you wearing? Use total physical response. Stand up. What are you doing? I am standing. Open the book. What are you doing? I am opening the book. Touch the wall. What are you doing? I am touching the wall. Use objects around students and parts of the body. Touch your head, arm, finger . . . Raise your hand. (shake, move, pull, bend, point) Nod your head . . .

3. Play "Simon Says" with students taking turns giving directions.

4. Compare students as examples of adjectives. Line up three students in front of class. Example: One is short. One is tall. One is shorter than the other. One is the shortest.

5. **Writing exercise**
Describe yourself:
    How old are you?
    Where are you from?
    Are you tall or short?
            fat or thin? (other adjectives from above)
            friendly or mean?
            interesting/boring/funny?
            pretty/handsome/beautiful?
    What are you wearing today?
Describe someone in your family: mother, father, sister, brother, cousin . . .
    How old is she/he? Is she/he tall or short, etc.?
Describe one class member.

6. Filling Out Papers

Tina: What's the matter?

Manuel: I can't stand it. There are so many papers in this country.

Tina: What do you mean?

Manuel: Well, I always fill out papers everywhere I go.

Kiet: I know. When I first came, I got my I-94 card.

Tina: What's that?

Kiet: That's for refugees.

Manuel: Oh, I got a green card and a social security card and a driver's license and . . .

Kiet: We all fill out an alien address report every January.

Manuel: I don't understand why.

Tools for Dialogue

1. Does Manuel like to fill out papers?
   What papers do refugees have?
   What papers does Manuel have?

2. What's an alien address report?
   Why do people fill out alien address reports?

3. When do you fill out papers? (at school, work, for social security, food stamps)
   When you came, what papers did you fill out? (I filled out . . . .)
   What papers do you have in your wallet?
   What papers do you need to come to the United States?

4. Why does the U.S. government need so many papers?
   Can you come to the U.S. without papers?
   Why do many people decide not to fill out the alien address report?

5. Is it hard to fill out papers? Who can help you?
   Do you think papers are necessary? Which ones? Why?

Practice

What's that?
What do you mean?
What's the matter?

Suggested Activities

1. Bring in different examples of forms that students should learn how to fill out: (alien address report, applications for social security, work, for enrollment).

2. Have students copy information from the cards in their wallets. Make sure they know last and first names, order of addresses, descriptions of what they look like.

NAME (Last in CAPS) (First) (Middle)	I AM IN THE UNITED STATES AS: ☐ Visitor ☐ Permanent Resident ☐ Student ☐ Other _____ (Specify)
COUNTRY OF CITIZENSHIP	DATE OF BIRTH	COPY NUMBER FROM ALIEN CARD A
PRESENT ADDRESS (Street or rural route) (City or Post Office) (State) (Zip Code)	
(IF ABOVE ADDRESS IS TEMPORARY) I expect to remain there _____ years _____ months	
LAST ADDRESS (Street or rural route) (City or Post Office) (State) (ZIP Code)	
I WORK FOR OR ATTEND SCHOOL AT: (Employer's Name or Name of School)	
(Street Address or rural route) (City or Post Office) (State) (ZIP Code)	
PORT OF ENTRY INTO U.S.	DATE OF ENTRY INTO U.S.	IF NOT A PERMANENT RESIDENT, MY STAY IN THE U.S. EXPIRES ON: (Date)
SIGNATURE DATE	

AR–11 (Rev. 3–21–79) N   GPO : 1979—O–288–512   **OMB Appvd. No. 43–RO038**

7. What Do You Want To Be?

June: What are you studying now?
Rafi: I'm studying English.
June: What do you want to study next semester?
Rafi: I want to study English and carpentry.
June: Oh, do you want to be a carpenter?
Rafi: Yes, I'm a cook now, but I want to be a carpenter. What do you do?
June: I'm a student.
Rafi: What are you studying?
June: I'm studying English. I want to study nursing.
Rafi: Oh, do you need English first?
June: Of course!

Tools for Dialogue

1. What is Rafi studying?
   What does he want to study?
   What does he want to be?
   Why is June studying?
   What does she want to study?

2. What does June need before she can study nursing?
   When do you need English in the United States?
   Do you always need English?
   When don't you need English?

3. What are you studying?
   What do you want to study next semester?
                                 next year?
                                 in two years?
   Do you need English to study other things?

4. Why are you studying English?
   Do you want to also speak your language?
   Do you think it's important to speak your first language in the U.S.?
   Are there many people here who speak your language?

5. Is it possible to get a job without speaking English? Which jobs?

Conversation Circle

What are you studying now?
What do you want to study next year, in two years, in five years?

What do you do now? (student, or your work)
What do you want to do next year, in two years, in five years?

Where do you live now?
Where do you want to live next year, in two years, in five years?

Practice

What do you want to be?

	dancer.
	carpenter.
	seamstress.
I want to be a	mechanic.
	painter.
	nurse.
	doctor.

	to study?
	to eat?
What do you want	to drink?
	to do tonight?
	to do in five years?

---

8. Education Circle

Tools for Dialogue

1. Who's in the picture?
   What are they doing?
   Who's the teacher?

2. Are they studying?
   Are they learning?
   Is this a classroom?

3. Does your class look like this?
   When do you sit in circles?
   Do you like to sit in a circle? Why? Why not?
   Do you like the teacher to sit with students?
   Do you like chairs in rows with the teacher in front? Why? Why not?

4. Why are you learning?
   Why do you come to class?
   Why do you listen to each other?

5. What do you learn from each other?
   What can you teach each other?
   What helps you learn English?
   What is a good teacher? Why do you think so?

Conversation Circle

1. Ask students, "What are you?" When they respond, "I'm a . . . ," ask, "Are you a teacher?" They'll invariably say no. Then ask, "What can you teach me? Can you teach me to cook Vietnamese food?"

   Keep asking, "What can you teach? Can you teach _____?"
   Then, "Are you a teacher? Why not? You can teach me _____."
   Ask, "Am I a teacher? I can teach you English."
   "I am your student when you teach me _____."

Practice

When	
	do you learn English?
	do you talk to each other?
	do you listen to each other?
	do you listen to the teacher?

Can you		
	speak English?	Yes, I can _____.
	ride a bicycle?	No, I can't _____.
	cook good food?	
	speak your language?	

II. FAMILY OVERVIEW

Language in Family unit presented in following lesson plans, codes 1–8:

Vocabulary: relatives (1)
missing people (1)
what people do every day (2)
housework (3)
childcare (4)
differences (5)

Language functions and structures:

express status (1) — I'm a widow.
express pleasure (2) — I like the morning.
(4) — That's great.
express displeasure (2) — I don't like it.
express sympathy (4) — That's too bad.
express preference (7) — I'd like to watch T.V.
(8) — Would you like to go out?
make invitation (8) — Can you come over?
give response (8) — Sure, maybe, not really.
use present, past, and habitual present tense (throughout)

Family means many different things to all of us. This unit addresses the many complex feelings about family, the confusions about expectations, and the differences in family lifestyles and needs. The majority of immigrant ESL students have families in two or more countries. Many have come to the U.S. under the Family Reunification category to join relatives. In doing so, however, they leave behind others. This process of leaving (and regaining) family can extend for many years and have disturbing emotional consequences. Many men immigrate alone and wait for years to bring wives, children, parents, or siblings. Many women who come alone (often to live with a relative) feel that their home is back where they came from.

While American culture exhibits a high degree of mobility, many ESL students come from a culture where family members live nearby, and participate closely in each other's lives. Separation from individual family members can cause considerable sadness, particularly if students are political refugees who can't return to visit those who stayed behind.

In the classroom, innocent questions might provoke this sadness unexpectedly. For example, we might ask a Hmong woman from Laos, "Are you married?" We would probably get an answer that we've taught—"Yes, I am," or "No, I'm not." But in Hmong culture, husbands may have many wives, and only one is permitted into the United States. This woman might be the first wife who was privileged to come, but her family unit has been broken in two. Asking "How many children do you have?" again might get only a partial answer. She might not count the ones who have died, been lost, or the ones left in the refugee camps.

Moving from one country to another is obviously difficult. People encounter different expectations in behavior, child-raising, and living proximity. These difficulties in adapting are compounded when people have left extended family structures which traditionally gave them support.

U.S.-born ESL students with extended families may have similar difficulties in interacting with the mainstream of American culture which places less value on close family ties. Many of these conflicts surface through discussions of child-raising. Students are disturbed that their children are becoming Americanized, with children showing less respect for older relatives or teenagers wanting to stay out late. Many worry about themselves becoming old in the U.S. without their family support. Sometimes people seek out friends, Anglo-Americans or people from the same culture, to become "like family."

The first dialogue begins with people explaining what family means to them. Students describe their family, who they live with, who lives in their home country, and their feelings about the separation. The vocabulary includes, "I'm a widow; I'm divorced," phrases not often included in ESL curriculum. One dialogue explores the loneliness some feel when they have little or no family in the U.S. and can't seem to make friends because of the language barrier.

Other dialogues examine male and female roles in the family, and child-raising issues, from the child care needed by single parents or working mothers to the problems of teenagers and dating. The dialogues on children lead into a discussion of family life: "What does a family do together; How do families help each other; What brings a family close together?" The sample unit closes with a dialogue on the role of friends helping and enjoying one another, or even becoming part of the family.

1. My Family

My name is Abdul. I live with my wife, Leila. We have two children, a son and a daughter. Daoud is two years old and Sandra is eight. My mother lives with us in my house. My grandmother lives nearby. My sister and her family live in Saudi Arabia. I'm sad they live far away. I miss them.

Tools for Dialogue

1. Does Abdul have children?
   How old is Daoud?
   How old is Sandra?
   Who lives in the house?
   Where does Abdul's grandmother live?

2. Where does her sister live?
   Why is Abdul sad?
   Who does Abdul miss?

3. Who lives in your house?
   In your family, who lives in the U.S.?
   Do they live nearby?
   Do you have family in another country? Where?
   Do you miss them?

4. Why did you move?
   Why didn't all of your family come with you?

5. Do you visit family in the U.S.?
   Do you visit family in your home country?
   Does your family visit you?
   Do you write letters? Do you send money?

Conversation Circle

Are you married? Are you single? Are you divorced? Are you widowed?
Do you have children? How old are they?
Do you want children?
Do you have brothers/sisters/aunts/uncles/grandmothers/grandfathers/nieces/
   nephews/cousins? How many do you have? How old are they? Where do
   they live?

Practice

Who do you miss?	I miss _____
Who does she miss?	She misses _____
Who does he miss?	He misses _____
Who do they miss?	They miss _____
Who do we miss?	We miss _____

Suggested Activities

1. Ask students, "What is family?"
2. Have students draw their family tree and fill in the names. Ask them to write sentences, i.e. I have two uncles. Their names are . . . .
3. On a world map, locate where families live with pins. Connect with colored threads.
4. Design an exercise for students to interview each other about family members (what they look like, where they live, etc.).
5. Have students bring in family photographs to share.

2. At Home Every Day

Selma: Every day, it's the same old thing.
Carlos: What do you mean?
Selma: The days always start the same.
Paulo: What do you do every day?
Selma: I get up at 7 o'clock. I wash my face and get dressed. Then I make breakfast at 7:30 for my husband and children.
Carlos: I like the morning. I drink my coffee slowly and read the newspaper before work.
Paulo: Me too. I like the morning.
Selma: You don't have to cook breakfast for your family.
Paulo: No, I don't have a family. I live alone.
Carlos: My wife makes breakfast before we go to work.
Paulo: Don't you know how to make breakfast?
Carlos: I don't know. I never make it.

Tools for Dialogue

1. What does Selma do every day?
   What does Carlos do in the morning?
   Does Paulo like the morning?
   Does Paulo have a family? Does he make breakfast?
2. What's the matter?
   Why does Selma make breakfast?
   Who makes breakfast for Carlos?
   Does Carlos know how to make breakfast?
   Why doesn't he make breakfast?
3. What do you do in the morning?
   Do you like the morning? Do you read the paper?
   Who makes breakfast?
   Do you know how to make breakfast?
4. Why do women make breakfast?
   When do men make breakfast?
5. Can men cook?
   Can men take care of the home?

Practice

I like the morning.
      the evening.

I
    get up.
    get home.
    get dressed.
    wash my face.
    brush my teeth.
    take a shower/a bath.
    make breakfast.
    cook dinner.

I don't like to get up.
            cook breakfast.

Writing Exercise

1. When do you get up?
   What do you do in the morning?
   When do you get dressed?
   Who makes breakfast?
2. When do you leave the house?
   Where do you go?
   When do you get home?
3. Who cooks dinner?
   What do you do in the evening?
   What do you do before bed?

Suggested Activities

1. Have students answer the following questions orally and on paper.

   What do you do in the   bedroom / kitchen / living room / dining room   every day?

   What room do you watch TV in?
   What room do you eat in?
   Where does your family eat?
   Where does your family sit and talk?
2. Have students role-play (with physical response) what people do in the morning; i.e. "I pick up my toothbrush, I put toothpaste on it, I lift it . . . ."

3. Housework

Tools for Dialogue

1. What is she doing?
   What is she ironing?
   What is the child doing?
   Where are the dishes?

2. Does she have a lot of work?
   Is she tired? How does she feel?
   Is housework hard work?

3. Who does the housework in your house?
   Are you tired after housework?
   Who helps in the house?

4. Why is she so tired?
   Why do housewives sometimes say, "I don't work"?
   Do housewives get paid?

5. Where's the husband?
   Can he help?
   Can men and women both do housework?
   Can men and women both take care of children?

Conversation Circle

What housework do wives do every day? What do you do?
What housework do husbands do? What do you do?
Do they do different things? Why?

What do boys do in the house?
What do girls do in the house?
Do boys and girls learn to do the same work at home?
Why not? What do you think about that?

In your home country, what do boys do at home?
                    what do girls do at home?
Are their jobs the same or different? Why?

Practice

	do housework	
	wash dishes	
	dry dishes	
	sweep floors	
	mop floors	
I	wash clothes	every day.
	iron clothes	
	set the table	
	cook dinner	
	take care of the house	
	take care of the children	
	take care of everything	

I don't . . . .
I don't like to . . . .

Writing Exercise

What housework do you do in the morning?
Who washes dishes?
Who dries dishes?
Who sweeps the floors?
Who mops the floors?
Who irons the clothes?
Who washes the clothes?
What housework do you do in the evening?

Who takes care of the children in the day?
Who takes care of the children in the evening?

4. Taking Care of Children

Marie: I'm tired. I had a long day at work.

Lucienne: I know. I work all day and then come home to three kids.

Sofie: You're lucky you have a husband.

Lucienne: Sometimes I am.

Sofie: It's better than no one.

Marie: My mother helps me. She takes care of Martin and Tony after school.

Sofie: That's great. I'm alone. Eliza stays in childcare until I come home from work.

Lucienne: That's a very long day.

Sofie: I know. But I'm lucky I have childcare.

Tools for Dialogue

1. Who is tired?
   Who has a long day at work? Marie? Sofie? Lucienne?
   Who does Lucienne live with?
   Who does Marie live with? Who helps her?
   Who does Sofie live with? Who helps her?

2. Why is Marie tired? Lucienne? Sofie?
   How many hours do they work?
   Do they work outside the house?
   Do they work inside the house?
   What do they do inside the house?
   Does Lucienne's husband help?
   Does Marie's mother help? What if her mother is sick?

3. Do you work outside the house? in the house?
   Do you have children?
   Who takes care of the children in the day?
   Who takes care of the children at night?
   How do you feel about your family taking care of the children?
   How do you feel about a friend? a neighbor?
   How do you feel about a childcare center?

4. Why is Sofie lucky?
   Why does she need childcare?
   Does everyone have family who can help?
   Do men take care of children?
   What can they do? What can't they do?
   When can family help? When can't they help?

5. Are there childcare centers near you?
   What are they like? Are they bilingual?
   What does a good center have?

   Are there many children on your street?
   Do mothers work?
   Who takes care of the children?
   How can you help each other?

Practice

I'm   lucky.
You're
She's
He's
We're
They're

          That's great.

I'm   not lucky.
You're
She's
He's
We're
They're

          That's too bad.

Suggested Activities

1. Have students talk about how their lives changed after their first child was born (if appropriate). How did their lives change? How does it feel to be a parent? Do they need help? Why?
2. Ask if any students take their children to day care. Share resources.
3. Bring in day care teacher and discuss resources within community, their availability, cost, differences in programs.
4. If there is concern, discuss issues in parenting. "What do you do with your children? What can your children do alone?"

5. Teenagers

It's hard to be a mother or father in the United States. Children here are so different than they are in my country. They grow up faster. They go out on dates alone. They know more. They don't listen. Sometimes we don't know what to do.

Tools for Dialogue

1. Who's in the picture?
   What is the teenager doing?
   How does the mother feel? How does the daughter feel?

2. Do you think children are different here?
   How are children different here?
   How are teenagers different here? How are dates different?

3. Are you different? How are you different?
   How does it feel to be a mother? A father?
   Who do you want your teenagers to date?
   Who do you want your children to marry?

4. Why are you different here?
   Is that good? Is that bad?
   Do you think it's hard to be a mother or father in the U.S.?

5. What do you want for your children?
   What do your children want?
   What do you want for yourself?
   Can you talk to your children or other children?
   How can you listen to each other?

Practice

Teenagers here grow up faster.
               go out alone.
               are different.

Teenagers here don't listen.
               go out with family.

Suggested Activities

1. Make a chart: *U.S.A.*   *My Country*
   a. How people dress
      (formal vs. informal)
   b. Teenage dates
   c. Parties
   d. What families do together
   e. Being on time
   f. etc.   Finish sentences: "In my country, we _____."
                       "In America it's different. In America we _____."
                 Fill in chart and discuss how people feel about differences.

2. Discuss different age groups, children to elderly. Where do they live? When do children leave home? Who takes care of old people?

3. Have students draw a life-cycle line for themselves in the U.S. vs. what life would be like in their home country.

6. Rolando Galang's Story

I came to the U.S. a few months ago. I live with my brother and his family. Every day I get up at 7 a.m., I catch a 7:30 bus to go to work. Every day I get on the same bus and see the same people, but no one says hello. I'm a mechanic. I work alone at my brother's shop. I don't have friends here. Sometimes the man from across the street comes over and works on the car with my brother. It's hard to meet people, especially Americans.

Tools for Dialogue

1. Who does Rolando live with?
   What does Rolando do every day?
   What is his work?
   Does he work alone?
   Does he have friends?
   Who comes over sometimes?

2. How does he feel about life here?
   Is he lonely?
   Is it hard for Rolando to meet people?

3. Who do you live with?
   Do you work alone? in the house? outside of the house?
   Do you have friends?
   Do you have American friends?
   Do you speak English with your friends?
   Is it hard for you to meet people here?

4. Why is it hard to meet people?
   Where do you meet other people from your country?
   Where do you meet Americans?

5. Can you tell someone in class where to meet people?
   Can you bring in information for anyone?

Practice

I live alone
   eat

             other people.
             friends.
   work   my family.
I live with my brother.
   eat   my sister.
             my parents.

Suggested Activities

1. Have students look on bulletin boards in neighborhoods or at school for things to do. Ask them to bring in information to share.
2. Bring in community calendars from community centers, schools, or the YMCAs and go over classes or open house nights with students.
3. Have students call a community center and ask for classes.
4. Have students role-play meeting someone and asking what's happening in the community.
5. Discuss where you meet people in the U.S. Ask students, "Is it hard to meet new people? Is it hard to have American friends? Where do you meet people?"

7. Family Life

Husband: Let's sit outside and watch the people.
  Wife: Are you crazy? Nobody sits outside here.
Husband: But remember how we always sat outside in the evening?
  Wife: That was in El Salvador.
Husband: Yes, but it's a warm summer evening.
  Wife: Let's watch T.V.
Husband: Oh, come on. I'd like to talk to you.
  Wife: All right. There's nothing good on T.V. tonight.

Tools for Dialogue

1. What does the husband want to do?
   Do people sit outside on the street?
   What does the wife want to do?
   What time of day is it? How hot is it?

2. Where do people sit outside?
   Can you talk and watch T.V.?

3. What does your family do together?
   Do you sit outside and watch people?
   How do you feel on your street?
   Did you sit outside in your home country?
   What did you like about life in your country?

4. Why are American streets different from your country?
   Is family life different? How? Why?

5. Would you like to sit outside? I'd like to _____.
   Would you like to talk to people on the street? I'd like to _____.
   Would you like to live close to other family members? I'd like to _____.

Conversation Circle

What do you do with your family?
Do you watch T.V., eat dinner, eat breakfast, study, go out together?
What do you like to do on summer evenings inside the house? Outside the
  house?
What did your family do together in your home country?
What do you do with your family when you go out? What do you do on
  Sundays?

Practice

I'd like to	watch people. eat dinner. go to a movie. talk with you.
Let's	sit outside. watch T.V. eat dinner. go to a movie.

Suggested Activities

1. Discuss the difference between family life in the U.S. and other countries. Start with questions on childhood for oral and written exercise. "When I was a child, I lived with, I studied, I worked at home, I helped my parents . . ."

2. Have students describe one day when they were seven, twelve, twenty years old. Use past tense of every day language. Ask when they first went to school, when they stopped going to school, when they first went to work.

3. Make a list on the board of what the students' mothers and fathers did. Then ask, "What did your parents want you to do, and what do you want your children to do?"

4. Bring in T.V. schedules. Ask what students' favorite programs are. Practice time: "My favorite program is on from _____ to _____. Ask why they like T.V. and what else they could do with their families.

8. Going Out

Kenji: Hello, Seiji and Mariko. How are you and the baby?

Seiji: We're okay. The baby's a little cranky.

Kenji: Do you want to go out tonight?

Mariko: Maybe, where would you like to go?

Kenji: I don't know. Would you like to eat out?

Seiji: Not really. It costs too much money.

Kenji: How about a movie?

Mariko: We would need a babysitter.

Seiji: Maybe your sister can take care of her. Do you want to call her?

Mariko: Sure, I'll call her.

Seiji: Wait, she has class tonight.

Kenji: Well, call a babysitter. We can all pay.

Tools for Dialogue

1. How does the baby feel?
   What does Kenji want to do?
   Does Seiji want to eat out?
   How much does it cost?

2. Can they go out?
   Do they need a babysitter?
   Who can take care of the baby?

3. Do you go out with your family?
   Do you go out with friends? Do you visit friends?
   Do you take your children? Where? When?
   Who takes care of your children when you go out?

4. Why don't you always take your children with you?
   Are babysitters expensive?

5. How do your friends help?
   Are they the same as family? Are some friends the same as family?
   How do women help each other?
   How do men help each other?

Conversation Circle

In your home country, do people go out with their children?
In the United States, do people go out with their children?
What do you like more to do? Why?

Practice

Would you like to _____?

Would she like to _____?

Would   he like to _____?

Would they like to _____?

Would we like to _____?

I'd like to _____.

She'd like to _____.

He'd like to _____.

They'd like to _____.

We'd like to _____.

Would you like to go to a movie?

How about a movie?

Sure, let's go to a movie.

Maybe. What's playing?

I don't know. What's playing?

Not really. Let's go to a party.

No. I wouldn't.

Suggested Activities

1. Discuss going to dinner at someone's house in America and in other countries. "Do you bring your children/babies with you? Do you bring a gift?" Have students role-play asking if they can bring their children.

2. Ask where students like to go when they go out. "Where can you go for free?"

3. Have students role-play dinner invitations: "Can you come for dinner tomorrow?" "I'd like to invite you for dinner tomorrow."

III. CULTURE AND CONFLICT OVERVIEW

Language in Culture and Conflict unit presented in following lesson plans, codes 1–8:

Vocabulary: culture (1)
           taking the bus (2)
           ordering in a restaurant (4)
           stereotypes (6)
           ethnic neighborhoods (7)
           names and nicknames (8)

Language functions and structures:

           give negative command (3) — Stop talking.
           express polite/impolite phrases (4)
           give apology (4) — Excuse me. I'm sorry.
           request clarification (4) — What did you say? Repeat that.
           offer help (4) — Can I help you?
           express gratitude (4)
           state opinion — agreement (5) — I think so.
                       — disagreement — I don't think so.

In the United States, both the new immigrant and U.S.-born non-English speaking minority experience conflict with the mainstream of American society. New immigrants are expected to suffer initial "culture shock," but these conflicts can be more long term than is commonly realized.

Access to jobs and education in the U.S. is limited for lower-class immigrants. Though many ESL students expect English to be the key to upward mobility, the barriers to advancement often generate frustrations. The frustrations coupled with the fear of losing their own culture and language can make learning English a potentially tense experience. Language motivation may drop as students withdraw into their ethnic communities.

This unit addresses the conflicts students feel when they interact with Anglo culture—the differences in values, traditions, and expectations for their children. To maintain their culture and lessen the conflicts, many cultural groups have created mutual aid societies, fraternal organizations, and social clubs. In addition, many have created institutions to teach their culture to their children.

Despite these programs, children of immigrant families rarely accept their parents' culture completely. Schools can seldom offer a full multicultural curriculum, and bilingualism in society is devalued. Many second-generation children from immigrant families do not speak the same language as their grandparents or parents.

As expected, when children grow up in the United States, they develop a mixture of cultural identities, challenging parents to reexamine a previous cultural purity. The longer immigrant groups live in America, the more adjustments they make. The diversity of identities, however, is greater than might be imagined.

In the case of those of Mexican ancestry, people identify themselves differently: Mexican, Mexican-American, Chicano, Pocho, Hispanic, Latino, Tejano. Many Mexicans call their U.S.-born children Mexican-American, but dislike the term Chicano. Others take pride in what they consider a uniquely Chicano culture. These diverse identifications can create conflicts even within a community, with some desiring cultural purity and some demanding acceptance of biculturality. In teaching ESL, cultural distinctions must be kept in focus.

This unit begins by asking people to define culture. Discussions encourage students to view themselves as *makers of culture*, contributing information on how they raise their children, live with their families, and earn a living. A first question, "What is culture?" would generate a long list: family, education, crafts, dance, music, religion, respect for elders, history, foods, and anything else students suggest.

Dialogues then discuss how culture changes when life situations change after people move into a new culture. Students explore the conflicts they and their children feel. A curriculum based on students' culture and their changes creates an atmosphere of mutual respect. As students see themselves as creators of culture, they can formulate an improved self-image which, in turn, helps resolve their conflicts about learning English and living in the United States.

1. What is Culture?

Tools for Dialogue

1. What's in the kitchen?
   What country are things from?
   What is the mother saying?
   What language is she speaking?
   What is the daughter saying?
   What language is she speaking?

2. Does the daughter speak Spanish?
   Does the daughter know how to make tortillas?
   Where was the daughter born?
   Does the mother speak English?
   Does the mother want the daughter to speak Spanish?
   How does the picture make you feel?

3. Do your children speak your language? When?
   Do their friends speak your language?
   What language do you speak at home?
   Do your children know how to cook food from your country?
   Do they celebrate the holidays?
   Do you want them to? Why?

4. How do your children learn about your country and language?
   Do they learn at home? at school?
   Do schools teach about your country?
   Do newspapers and television talk about your country? What do they say?

5. Do you want schools to teach about your country?
   Do you think T.V. should talk about your country?
   Can you teach your children's teachers about your country (holidays,
   history, culture)?
   How can you teach people?

Suggested Activities

1. Make a list on the board of answers to the question, "What is culture?"
   Include all facets: music, art, language, customs, religion, values, holidays,
   family, making a living. Ask what's important to keep in America.

2. Have students bring in objects they have made (arts, crafts, utensils,
   tools) from their country. Ask them to describe how they made it: "How
   long does it take? What do you need to make it? Do you teach your
   children how to make it? How did you learn? How do you feel about
   what you made? Are you proud?"

3. Ask students to describe their kitchens or other rooms that have objects
   from their country. Devise a conversation and writing exercise:

   What do you have in your kitchen from your country?
   What do you have in your house from your country?
   What handmade things do you have?
   Where are they from?
   Did you make them?
   What do you have in your kitchen from the United States?
   What foods do you cook from your country?

4. Have students ask you as the teacher:

   What do you have in your kitchen?
   What handmade things do you have? Where are they from?
   What foods do you cook?
   How is your kitchen/house different from my kitchen/house?

2. Getting Around

Antonio: Excuse me. I need to go to Second Avenue.

Bus driver: Yes, this bus goes to Second Avenue. Move in, please.

Antonio: How much?

Bus driver: It's sixty cents. You need exact change.

Antonio: Here's one dollar.

Bus driver: You need exact change.

Antonio: What?

Bus driver: Don't you know English? It's sixty cents. Move in please!

Passenger: Excuse me. Can I help you?

Antonio: How much?

Passenger: You have a dollar? I think I have change. Here.

Antonio: Thank you.

Passenger: Drop sixty cents in the coin slot. Here. Are you new here?

Antonio: Yes, I'm from Puerto Rico.

Tools for Dialogue

1. Where does Antonio need to go?
   How much is the bus?
   Does he have exact change?
   Who helps him?

2. Where is Antonio from? Is he American?
   Is he nervous? Does he know what to do?
   How does the conversation make you feel?
   How long does it take to learn English?

3. Are you comfortable on buses?
   When are you nervous in the U.S.?
   When are you nervous speaking English? speaking on the phone? at the
   doctor's? at stores? . . .

4. Why are you nervous speaking English?
   Are people sometimes unfriendly?
   Is it hard or easy to speak English?

5. Can you ask for help?
   Can you help other people? How?

Suggested Activities

1. Have students role-play asking for help and information—"Can you help me, please?" and offering help—"Can I help you?"

2. List on board situations in which students need to speak English, and when they need to understand English. Ask what they can do if they are nervous.

3. Practice mini-dialogues of telephone conversations: asking the operator for a number, asking if someone is home, asking for an appointment at offices. Have students call each other during week. Have students call TIME, the WEATHER, the operator for information, and public offices for information. Then ask for reports in class.

4. Bring in phone books to familiarize students with looking up information. Let students know that often there are bilingual phone operators who can help them. Ask if they think phone operators should speak their language. Ask, "What if there's an emergency? Are there many people in your city who speak your language?"

3. Languages in a Classroom

Tools for Dialogue

1. Where is the teacher?
   What are Chandee and Bouachanh doing?
   What is the teacher saying?
   Where are Chandee and Bouachanh from?

2. Does the teacher speak Laotian?
   Does the teacher respect the children?
   Why does she tell them to speak English?
   How do you feel about the teacher?

3. What language do you speak at home?
   Do you want your children to speak your language?
   Do your children's teachers speak your language?
   Do you want them to?

4. Do your children sometimes not want to speak your language? Why?
   Are they embarrassed? Why?
   Why do teachers tell children to speak English?

5. Can schools teach English and let children speak their language also?
   What do you think about bilingual classes?
   What do you think about bilingual teachers?
   Would you like your children to speak English and their language at
      school?
   Are there many people from your country in the United States?

Conversation Circle

What do you think about bilingual classes?
What do you think about the teacher in the picture?
What do you think about this class?
What do you think about your job?
What do you think about the United States?

Practice

Stop	whispering.
	talking.
	eating in class.

Don't	whisper, please.
	talk, please.

Be quiet, please.

I think . . . .

What *does she* think ———————?
    does he
    do you
    do they
She thinks ———————————.
He thinks ———————————.

Suggested Activities

1. Have students role-play a conference between a teacher and parents about a child who doesn't want to speak English.

2. Have students role-play a parent/teacher conference about a child's progress. Help them develop questions that parents would ask teachers and vice versa before the role-play.

3. Bring in a summary of the bilingual education code, or Lau vs. Nichols case to talk about bilingual education rights.

4. Discuss students using their first language when they're learning English —when it helps and when it doesn't.

4. In a Fast-Food Restaurant

Waitress: Hello, is this for here or to go?

Juana: For here.

Waitress: Are you ready to order?

Juana: Yes please. We'd like two enchiladas, a hamburger, and my mother wants a burrito.

Waitress: I'm sorry. What did you say?

Jorge: Two enchiladas, a hamburger, and a burrito.

Waitress: Oh, you mean two "enchahladas," a hamburger, and a "buhrido."

Juana: Yes please.

Waitress: What would you like to drink?

Jorge: Excuse me. What did you say, please?

Waitress: Never mind. Do you want soda?

Jorge: Yes, two Cokes and what do you want, mamá?

Mother: Let's go home.

Juana: Oh, mamá. Don't you want pineapple juice?

Waitress: There are other people waiting. Could you hurry it up?

Juana: She wants pineapple juice.

Waitress: We have Coke, Seven-Up, and orange drink.

Jorge: Okay. Three Cokes please.

Waitress: Thank you. I'll bring your drinks first.

Tools for Dialogue

1. What do they order?
   Does the waitress understand Juana?
   Does the waitress speak Spanish?

2. Does the mother like the restaurant? Why not?
   Is the waitress friendly? polite?
   What does she say that is polite? impolite?

3. How do you feel when people don't understand you?
   How do you feel when people don't speak your language?
   How do you feel when people are impolite?

4. Do you think everyone needs to speak English? Why or why not?
   Do you want other people to speak your language?

5. What do you say when you don't understand?
   What do you say when people don't speak your language correctly?
     Can you teach them?
   What do you say when someone is impolite?

Suggested Activities

1. Write down the waitress' polite and impolite sentences. Discuss. Think of others.

2. Role-play polite and impolite encounters. "What do you say?"
   Show with drawings and actions:
   a) Apologies—bump into someone, late to class, spill drink. (I'm sorry. Excuse me.)
   b) Not understanding—(Can you repeat that? Repeat that please. I don't understand. What did you say, please? Wait a minute. Talk slower.)
   c) Helping someone—(Can I help you? May I help you?)
   d) When someone doesn't understand you—(Let me repeat that. I'll repeat.)
   e) Thanking someone—(Thank you. You are kind. That was nice of you.)

3. Oral and writing exercise:

   What do you say if
   - you don't understand someone?
   - you want someone to repeat something?
   - you want someone to speak more slowly?
   - someone talks loudly?
   - someone is impolite?
   - someone doesn't understand you?

5. More Restaurants

Menus

American

Chinese

Dinners with Soup & Salad		Sandwiches			Dinner	Lunch
Steak Dinner	$5.50	hamburger	$2.25	Chicken Chow Mein	$3.25	$2.50
Broiled Fish	4.30	cheeseburger	2.75	Cashew Chicken	4.50	3.50
Spaghetti	3.95	turkey	3.00	Sweet and Sour Pork	4.50	3.25
Beef Stew	4.25	grilled cheese	2.25	Shrimp and vegetables	4.25	3.50
Chicken	4.50	tuna	2.75	Assorted vegetables	4.00	3.00
				Beef, green peppers		
		omelet	3.75	and mushrooms	4.75	3.50
		2 eggs/toast	2.50	Egg Foo Yung	3.50	2.25
tossed green salad	$1.50	milk	$ .40	Pork fried rice	1.50	—
potato salad	.75	beer	1.00	Steamed rice	.40	—
soup of the day		coffee	.40	Fried won ton	2.25	1.50
and bread	2.00	tea	.30	Wonton soup	3.25	1.95

Choose a lunch or dinner from the menu. Write down your order.

Conversation Circle

When do you like to eat at a restaurant?
When do you like to eat at home?
Is it expensive to eat out?
Where do you like to eat out?
What food do you like to eat?
What American food do you like? What don't you like?
What other foods do you like?

Suggested Activities

1. Use these menus or bring in real menus. Have students practice in groups of three, ordering and writing down orders for lunch or dinner. Then present to the rest of the class. Have them calculate prices. "How much can you spend for breakfast, lunch, or supper? How much do you spend in your country? How much are tips?"

2. Have students make up a menu for restaurants in their home countries.

3. Ask students to role-play a family of tourists ordering dinner in their home country. "How do you feel? How does the family feel?"

4. Ask students to role-play being overcharged for supper. What do they say?

5. Prepare for a field trip to a restaurant.

6. Ask students to share a recipe from their country with the other students.

7. Ask students, "How do you get a waiter's attention in a restaurant here? In your home country, how do you get a waiter's attention?" "What is polite in America? What is impolite in America?"

8. How do you decide who pays in the U.S.? In your country? What's "going Dutch"?

6. Stereotypes

List some stereotypical sentences on the board, or bring in pictures depicting stereotypes. (You can start the list and have students contribute.)

Ask: What are Mexicans like?
    What are Vietnamese like?
    What are Americans like?   Arabs? Chinese? Philipinos?
                                 Blacks? Puerto Ricans?
                                 Dominicans? Men? Women?

Tools for Dialogue

1. What is a stereotype?
   Who has stereotypes?
2. Are stereotypes true? Why or why not?
   Are they always true? Why or why not?
3. Do you have stereotypes? Do your children believe in stereotypes?
   What do you think of . . . (different peoples)?
   Do you know people from other cultures? Do you know . . . (different ethnic/racial groups)?
4. Where do stereotypes come from? Who makes them up?
   Do stereotypes hurt people? How?
   Are people sometimes afraid of other groups? Why?
5. How can we stop stereotypes?
   How can we know other peoples?
   What stops us from knowing other people?
   Where can you meet people from other cultures?

Suggested Activities

1. Ask students what stereotypes of Americans they may have had before immigration. What do they think now? Are some true?

2. Compare stereotypes of men and women in different cultures. Ask, "How are men and women thought of in your culture? How are men and women thought of in America?"

3. Oblongs that look like bricks can be made from paper or cards. On the "bricks," write words that often cause feelings of fear, isolation, or other attitudes which create or perpetuate stereotypes (ignorance, prejudice, embarassment, dislike, no contact, fear, invisibility, impatience, missing facts . . .). Discuss when students experience these feelings. When do other people (Americans and other groups) experience these attitudes? Have people construct a paper brick wall and have everyone push against it to knock it down. (Paper brick wall developed by multicultural puppeteer Camy Condon.)

7. Cultural Neighborhoods

In the United States, there are immigrants and refugees from countries and cultures all over the world. Many people live in mixed neighborhoods. Others live in separate or ethnic neighborhoods like Chinatowns. Why do people live in different neighborhoods?

Tools for Dialogue

Note: Write the words *ethnic* (segregated or separate) and *mixed* (integrated) on board. Discuss their meanings before starting the lesson.

1. What neighborhood is this?
   What language do people speak?
   What do you see in a Chinese neighborhood?
   Is this an ethnic neighborhood?

2. Why do Chinese people live in Chinatown?
   Where is it cheap to live?
   Where is it expensive to live?

3. Do you live in a mixed (or integrated) neighborhood?
   Do you live in an ethnic (or segregated) neighborhood?
   What languages do people speak in your neighborhood?
   Do many people speak your language there?
   What groups live in your neighborhood? Do you know them?
   What restaurants or stores are in your neighborhood?
   Why do you live there? Are you near family?
   Can you speak your language on the street?
   Are rents the right price?

4. Do you think people have a free choice about where they live?
   Why do some people live in mixed or integrated neighborhoods?
   Why do some people live in ethnic or segregated neighborhoods?
   Do some people feel uncomfortable in English-speaking neighborhoods? Why?

5. Where would you like to live?
   What do you like about mixed neighborhoods?
   What do you like about ethnic neighborhoods where people are from your culture?

Suggested Activities

1. Have students describe neighborhoods in their city (languages, stores, peoples). Ask what they see in a Mexican neighborhood, in a Japanese neighborhood, in a Cuban neighborhood.

2. Make a list of foods, words and expressions, sports, arts, etc., that have come from other cultures and are now part of American life.
   What parts of American culture have become part of your country?

8. Culture and Family

I am called Concha. My name is really Concepcion Maria Espinosa. All the girls in our family have the middle name of Maria. But no one calls me by my full name. I use Concha. It's easy to remember.

A lot of my friends were born in Mexico. They tease me by calling me "Pocha." Pocha means half-and-half Mexican but born in the United States. Pocha usually means you are not a good Mexican or a good American. It's not a nice word to be called. I don't like it. I prefer to be called Chicana—a Mexican-American.

My older sister, Isabel, calls herself Mexican. She only speaks Spanish. My mother and father call themselves Mexican. But I say I am a Chicana. That's our generation gap.

Tools for Dialogue

1. Where was Concha born?
   Where were a lot of her friends born?
   What do they call her?
   Does she like it?
   What does she like to be called?

2. What does "Pocha" mean?
   Why does Concha prefer to be called "Chicana"?
   What does "Chicana" mean to her?

3. Where were you born? Are you an immigrant?
   What nationality do you call yourself?
   What do you call your children? Are they immigrants?
   Are you different from your children? How?
   Are you different from your parents? How?

4. How is Asian-American different from Asian?
   How is Chinese-American different from Chinese?
   How is Filipino-American different from Filipino?
   How is Japanese-American different from Japanese?
   How is Cuban-American different from Cuban?
   How is Italian-American different from Italian?
   Why do you think there's a generation gap?

5. What do you want to keep from your culture?
   What do you want your children to keep?

Practice

What do your friends call you?
parents
children

    They call me . . . .

What does your mother call you?
father
daughter

    He/She calls me . . . .

I like to be called . . . .
I prefer to be called . . . .

What do *you* call *yourself*?
    does she call herself?
    does he call himself?
    do they call themselves?
    do we call ourselves?

    I call *myself* _____.

    She calls herself _____.

    He calls himself _____.

    They call themselves _____.

    We call ourselves _____.

Suggested Activities

1. Ask students, "What's your nickname? What do your friends/parents/ sisters call you?" "What nationality are you?"
2. Have students talk and write about any of their own experiences similar to Concha's. Is there a generation gap in any of their families? Who is involved? How can it be resolved?

IV. NEIGHBORHOODS OVERVIEW

Language in Neighborhoods unit presented in following lesson plans, codes 1-8:

Vocabulary:　prepositions (1)
　　　　　　　comparison words (2)
　　　　　　　house and neighborhood descriptions (2)
　　　　　　　directions when lost (3)
　　　　　　　renting a house (4)
　　　　　　　home repairs (5)

Language functions and structures:

express preference (3) — I like, I don't like.
express past preference (6) — I liked, I didn't like.
express requirement (3) — I have to _____.
request information (3) — Can you tell me _____.
give command (4)
express intention (5) — I'll help you.
express future intention (6) — I'm going to help.
make suggestion (7) — Let's, Why don't we _____.
　　　　　　　　　(8) — Maybe we should _____.
express hostility (8) — It's terrible.

A neighborhood is defined by economic and geographic boundaries which can also encompass social identification and an emotional sense of home, belonging, and the fear of intrusion. Americans idealize "the neighborhood" as a stable place where people know the families next door, yet maintain individual privacy.

Many neighborhoods where ESL students live, however, fall short of this ideal. ESL students often live in transitional areas with affordable rents, but dilapidated houses. The Tenderloin in San Francisco, for example, in 1981 had the largest concentration of Indochinese refugees in the city. Within a half-mile square, 10,000 refugees reside alongside 10,000 other residents in a high drug, high crime area. The housing shortage, drain on social services, and the inability to communicate in the same language create tensions between residents. Other students live in ethnic neighborhoods for language security, but still have poor housing and services and crowded living conditions. Historically, language and economic discrimination have created what can be called "language ghettos," to which newer immigrants still head. Most immigrants seek the path of least resistance and conflict when they enter the United States. They want to settle where they can speak their language in stores, where social services may have bilingual/bicultural personnel, and where they can get jobs, including off-the-books employment. Immigrants often stay with relatives until they can manage on their own. Thus the language ghettos provide a home base and a way to maintain their cultural heritage.

This unit examines people's feelings about their neighborhood, what they like and what they'd like to change. Before beginning the dialogues, the question, "What is a neighborhood?" will elicit vocabulary and touch on the themes that appear later. The first dialogue starts with description during which students talk about their homes, how they feel about their neighborhoods, why they live there, what they like, what they don't like, etc.

Students then map out areas, learn the layout of the city, how to ask for and give directions, locate social services and stores, and become more confident in venturing into previously unknown areas. They talk about why neighborhoods differ as to services, cleanliness, and safety.

Students also focus on landlord/tenant relations—how to find a place to live, how to ask questions of landlords, and how to protect their rights as tenants.

If students are involved in specific projects such as organizing a childcare center or tenants union, they can share their information. Teachers can also provide resource information about city-wide or neighborhood groups and agencies that handle concerns expressed in the classroom. Even role-playing actions such as organizing a block meeting or writing a petition to City Hall give students the confidence to participate actively in the U.S.

Students are asked to compare their neighborhoods with those in their home countries, and finally, the unit ends on a hopeful note with students reexamining their neighborhoods' problems and what they can do to create better living situations and feelings of community.

1. My Home

Teresa: Hi, Silvia. Let's go to my house.
 Silvia: Okay. Where do you live?
Teresa: I live *in* Union City *at* 2734 Manila Road.
 Silvia: Do you live in an apartment?
Teresa: No, it's a house *on* Manila Road.
 Silvia: Do you own your house?
Teresa: No, we rent. Where do you live?
 Silvia: I live *at* 56 Porter Street, number 22.
Teresa: Oh, that's near me.
 Silvia: Yes, but we want to move. It's too noisy.

Tools for Dialogue

1. Where does Teresa live?
   Does she rent her house?
   Where does Silvia live?
   Does she rent her apartment?

2. Why does Silvia want to move?
   What are the problems with apartments?

3. Where do you live?
   Do you rent or own?
   Is your home small or big?
   Is it crowded? Is it noisy?
   What rooms are there?
   Are the walls thick or thin?
   How old is your home?
   Is it cheap or expensive to live in?

4. What do you like about your home?
   What don't you like?
   Why do you live there?

5. Do you want to move?
   Do you want to stay?
   Do you want to change anything?
   Can you move?

Conversation Circle

Where do you live? I live *in* (a city, the country, the suburbs)
in (an apartment, a house, a duplex, a housing project)
near/far from (stores, hospital, clinic, work . . .)

Practice

Where do you live?

I live
in (a city) _____.
on (a road) _____.
at (complete address) _____.

I live
near
far from
in front of   the school.
behind

Suggested Activities

1. List adjectives on the board (*pretty/ugly, old/new, small/big,* etc.) and have students compare their homes.
2. Bring in pictures of different living situations to compare and discuss.
3. Draw rooms of homes on the board. Teach vocabulary and have students describe their rooms and furniture. Ask what they do in the different rooms.

2. My Neighborhood

Rudy: Hello, Sam. Hello, Irma.
 Irma: Hello, neighbor.
Rudy: Can you help me?
 Sam: Maybe. How can we help?
Rudy: I want to put up a fence.
 Irma: A fence. What for?
Rudy: Oh, you know. There are so many dogs in the neighborhood.
 Sam: Yes, it's a problem!
 Irma: I know, but I don't like fences.

Tools for Dialogue

1. What does Rudy want?
   Can Sam and Irma help?

2. What's the problem?
   Does Irma like fences?

3. Do you know your neighbors?
   Do you help your neighbors? How?
   Do your neighbors help you?
   Do you like fences? Why? Why not?

4. Do you have dogs in your neighborhood?
   Are they a problem?
   What problems do you have?
   What do you like about your neighborhood?
   What don't you like?

5. What do you want to change?
   How can you change what you don't like?
   Are there neighborhood organizations?

Conversation Circle

What do you like in your neighborhood?
What don't you like in your neighborhood?
Who lives in your neighborhood?
What do you do in your neighborhood?

What languages are spoken in your neighborhood?
Why do you live there?
Where does the rest of your family live?

Practice

My neighborhood is	empty/crowded. clean/dirty. rich/poor. quiet/noisy. safe/dangerous. hilly/flat.
There are	street signs. public services. private houses. too many dogs. not enough buses.

I like/don't like . . . .
My children like/don't like . . . .

Suggested Activities

1. Have students draw a map of their neighborhood, starting with their homes, streets, nearby stores, schools, laundromats, playgrounds, parks, services, local hangouts, street signs. Ask where they eat, shop, play, etc. Ask them to write what they like and don't like. Ask them to describe what's important to them in their neighborhood.

2. Use a city street map to locate students' neighborhoods. Draw boxes around them and have students describe them.

3. Walk through the neighborhood around school and have students write down the words on signs. Have students take pictures of their neighborhood or the school area.

4. Bring in slides and pictures of different neighborhoods. Ask why people live there.

5. Have students compare their neighborhood with the city or rural area they used to live in.

3. I'm Lost

Huyhn: Excuse me, I'm lost. Can you tell me how to get to Alemany College?

Sang: I'm sorry. I'm new here also. Ask the woman across the street.

Huyhn: Excuse me. Can you tell me how to get to Alemany College?

Kit: Yes, you have to take two buses. Catch the number 14 at the corner and transfer to number 47 at Van Ness.

Huyhn: Where do I catch the bus?

Kit: Go straight down this street. Turn left at the corner. The bus stop is across the street in front of the liquor store.

Huyhn: Can you repeat that please? I didn't understand it all.

Kit: Sure, turn left at the corner. The bus stop is in front of the liquor store and across the street.

Huyhn: Thank you very much.

Tools for Dialogue

1. Is Huyhn lost?
   How many buses does Huyhn have to take?
   How can he catch the bus?

2. Is Huyhn new?
   Did he understand the directions?
   Does he need to get to school?
   What does he need to know to get to school?

3. Are you new here?
   Do you know the bus route(s) in your neighborhood?
   Where's the bus stop?
   What tells you it's a bus stop?
   How do you get to school?

4. Were you ever lost?
   How did you feel?
   What did you do?
   Did you ask for help?

5. What can you do if you are lost?
   What can you do if you don't understand?
   What can you do if you need help?

Practice

I   + verb
   You have to
They/We
   She/He *has to*

                          get to school?
                          catch a bus?
Can you tell me how to   cook rice balls?
                          say hello in your language?

Turn right at the corner.
Turn left at the stop sign.
Go straight.

Suggested Activities

1. Practice turning right and left using aisles in the classroom, with first the teacher giving directions and then the students telling each other.

2. Have students use a bus or subway map to tell each other how to get to various places.

3. Have students use their neighborhood maps to give each other walking directions and bus directions in and out of neighborhoods.

4. Have students tell each other how to get to school or work.

5. Have students role-play being lost and asking directions. Build neighborhood services vocabulary, e.g., "Excuse me, I'm lost. Can you tell me how to get to the laundromat/post office/legal aid office?"

6. Bring in bus schedules for students to read.

4. Renting a Home

Alvaro: Nanoy, do you know the city well?

Nanoy: I think so. Why?

Sabina: We want to find an apartment.

Nanoy: Where do you want to live?

Alvaro: Well, we have two young children. We want to live near a school.

Sabina: And near a grocery store. We don't have a car.

Nanoy: You can look in the newspaper in the classified ad section.

Alvaro: I don't speak English very well on the phone.

Sabina: Where do people speak Tagalog?

Nanoy: In this neighborhood. Look for "For Rent" signs.

Alvaro: Then what do I do?

Nanoy: Knock on the door and ask for the manager.

Sabina: Then what?

Nanoy: Ask if an apartment is still for rent. Ask how much it is and if they allow children.

Alvaro: How much are rents? We don't have a lot of money.

Nanoy: Rents are expensive here, more than in the Philippines.

Tools for Dialogue

1. Where do Sabina and Alvaro want to live?
   Do they have a car?
   How can they find an apartment?
   What do they ask the manager?
   What language do they speak?

2. How does Alvaro feel about speaking English on the phone?
   What neighborhood do they want to live in?
   Do they want to speak Tagalog in their neighborhood?
   How much rent can they pay?

3. Where do you live?
   How did you find your apartment/house?
   What did you ask the manager or landlord?
   Do you have what you need?
   What do you want?

4. Is your rent a lot of money?
   How much are rents in your city?
   Why are rents so expensive?
   Are there enough homes for everyone here?

5. What can you do about expensive rents?
   Can you ask your landlord or manager for cheaper rent?
   Is there a tenants' association in your city?

Practice

      What's
  How much is the rent please?
Can you tell me

    Knock on the door.
    Talk to the manager.
    Ask for the price.
    Order some coffee.
    Buy a newspaper.

Suggested Activities

1. List on board the questions to ask landlords or managers (include rent, cleaning and security deposits, if utilities are included, if pets and children are allowed).

2. Have students bring in want ads from the newspaper; help them decipher the abbreviations.

3. Have students role-play an interview with an apartment manager or landlord.

5. Home Repairs

Lilac: Hey, the roof is leaking.

Sum: Oh, no! Put a pail under it.

Lilac: Call Mr. Jones, the landlord.

Sum: Why? He won't fix it.

Lilac: Yes, he will. The lease says he repairs the building.

Sum: Let's call a repair person.

Lilac: How do we find someone?

Sum: Look in the yellow pages under roof repair.

Lilac: I'll keep the bill. The landlord will pay.

Sum: I hope so, but I don't think so.

Tools for Dialogue

1. What's the matter?
   Is it raining?
   Will the landlord fix it?
   How does Lilac find a repair person?

2. Will the landlord pay?
   What does the lease say?
   What happens if he doesn't pay?

3. Will your landlord or landlady make repairs?
   What will they fix?
   What do you fix at home?
   Who helps you?
   What will your landlord pay for?
   What does your lease say?

4. Do you have a lease or rental agreement?
   Did you read it before you signed it?
   Did you make any changes?

5. What happens if you don't pay the rent?
   What happens if your landlord doesn't pay for repairs?
   Who can you call for help?

Writing Exercise

1. When your roof is broken, who do you call?
2. When your stove is broken, who do you call?
3. When your phone is broken, who do you call?
4. When your sink is broken, who do you call?
5. When your fence is broken, who do you call?
6. When your television is broken, who do you call?

Practice—future

I	I	
You	You	
He	He	
She	will	She	won't/will not
We	We	
They	They	

I'll
You'll
He'll
She'll
They'll
We'll

	pay for it.
	keep the bill.
I'll	call the roofer.
	fix it.
	help you. . . .

Suggested Activities

1. Have students bring in telephone books to look up the numbers and addresses of repair people in or close to their neighborhoods.
2. Have students role-play phoning repair people and asking for prices of service.
3. Bring in a sample lease or rental agreement. Have students bring in theirs. Discuss rights and responsibilities of tenants and landlords.
4. Invite a member of a Tenants' Association or of the city housing office to discuss the law.
5. If appropriate, develop a code on a tenants' strike.

6. My Neighborhood in My Home Country

José Miguel: Hi, Gonzalo. How are you?

Gonzalo: I'm fine. How are you?

José Miguel: I'm fine, but I have a problem. I'm going to help my brother build an adobe house, but I don't know how.

Gonzalo: I can help you.

José Miguel: Thanks a lot. What do we need?

Gonzalo: We need a pick, a shovel, a wheelbarrow, and molds.

Rita: Good morning, Gonzalo. Good morning, José Miguel. What are you doing?

José Miguel: We're going to help my brother build an adobe house.

Rita: I know how to make adobe. Do you need help. I have a donkey.

Gonzalo: Do you know where we can get dry grass?

Rita: Yes, I do. We also need water.

Gonzalo: Okay, bring everything. We'll see you in an hour.

Tools for Dialogue

1. What are Gonzalo and José Miguel going to do?
   Does José Miguel know how to make adobe?
   What do they need?
   Is Rita going to help?

2. Do people build their own houses in your home country?
   What are the houses made of?
   How many people do you need to build a house?
   Who helps?

3. Do you know how to make adobe? How long does it take?
   Do you know how to build a house?
   Did you build your house in your home country?
   How did you build it?
   Who helped you?

4. Who builds houses here?
   Do you need a permit here?
   Do you need a permit in your home country?
   Do people help each other there?
   Do people help each other here?

5. Can people build their own houses in the U.S.?
   Can people own their houses together?

Conversation Circle

What was your neighborhood like in your home country? What did you like about it? What didn't you like?

How is your neighborhood here different? What do you miss? What would you like to see here?

Practice

	help my brother.
	eat out tomorrow.
I'm going to	study English.
	go shopping.
	read the paper.

Suggested Activities

1. List on the board what houses are made of in different countries (grass, adobe, wood, steel, concrete). Compare urban and rural living.

2. Bring in pictures of neighborhoods from many countries. Have students identify what they like and what they would like to see in the U.S.

3. Have students draw and describe the neighborhood they grew up in. Have students draw and describe the neighborhood they live in now.

7. What's Happening in My Community?

Luis: Say, I hear there's an open house Saturday at the senior center.
Omar: How do you know?
Luis: The local radio station. They broadcast in Spanish at certain hours.
Sara: Don't you listen to news in English?
Luis: Sometimes, but I like to hear news in Spanish, too.
Omar: I don't always understand the English, but I try.
Sara: So, what's happening?
Luis: It's a party. Organizations will talk about the neighborhood.
Omar: Which ones?
Luis: I don't know.
Sara: Maybe the newspaper has information.
Omar: Let's go to the center and look at the bulletin board.
Luis: Why don't we go and ask?

Tools for Dialogue

1. What's happening Saturday?
   How does Luis know?
   Does Luis listen to news in English?
   Where do they get information?

2. How do you learn about your community?
   How do you learn if you don't speak English?

3. Which radio station do you listen to?
   Do you listen to news in English?
   Do you listen to news in your language?
   What newspaper do you read?
   Where are the bulletin boards in your neighborhood?

4. Do you need information in your language?
   How can you get information in your language?
   Is it hard to get information in your language? Why?

5. Who can help you?
   How can you help someone who doesn't speak English?
   What community services can you tell someone about?
   What community services do you want to know more about?

Conversation Circle

How do you find the Med-i-caid office?
How do you find the community clinic?
How do you find the food stamp office?
How do you find an ESL class?
How do you find out what's happening in the community? Who do you ask?

Practice—suggestions

	go	_____ .
Let's	look	_____ .
	listen to	_____ .
	read	_____ .

	go there	_____ ?
Why don't we	look	_____ ?
	ask	_____ ?

Suggested Activities

1. Bring in (and ask students to bring in) notices from the local newspaper about what's happening in the community (services and entertainment).
2. Ask people to look at bulletin boards and report on information they collected.
3. Have students bring in phone books and look up city social services.
4. Have students role-play phone calls to social services offices. They should ask for hours, available services, special events.
5. Develop a radio spot in English telling about a special event.

8. Community Organizing

> Mrs. Lee: Good morning, Mr. Samuel. I'm your neighbor from down the block.
>
> Mr. Samuel: Good morning. What can I do for you?
>
> Mrs. Lee: I have a petition for City Hall. We want more street lights.
>
> Mr. Samuel: No thanks. I don't sign anything.

> Mrs. Lee: Good morning, Mrs. Patel. I have a petition for City Hall.
>
> Mrs. Patel: Oh, what for?
>
> Mrs. Lee: It's for more street lights. We think that this block is too dark and dangerous.
>
> Mrs. Patel: I think so, too. I never take a walk at night. It's horrible.
>
> Mrs. Lee: I know. I think lights will help.
>
> Mrs. Patel: Maybe. Anyhow, it's nice to meet a neighbor.
>
> Mrs. Lee: Yes, and after this petition we're going to have a block meeting.
>
> Mrs. Patel: Oh, when is it? I'll bring cookies.

Tools for Dialogue

1. What does the petition say?
   Does Mr. Samuel sign the petition? Why not?
   Is the street dark?
   Does Mrs. Patel walk at night?
   What's a block meeting?

2. What are the problems on this block?
   Will lights help?
   How will the block meeting help?

3. Is your street dark and dangerous?
   Do you walk at night? Is it safe?
   Do you know people on the block?
   What are the problems on your block?
   Do you sign petitions?
   Have you signed a petition before?

4. Why are there problems on the block?
   Why aren't there street lights?
   Why doesn't the city pay for lights?

5. Are there organizations on your block?
   Do you have block meetings? Who lives on your block?
   If you have a city problem, who can you complain to?
   Can you organize a block meeting?
   How do you organize a block meeting?

Practice

Maybe we should	get to know our neighbors.
	have a meeting.
	write a petition.

It's	horrible.
	terrible.
	dangerous.

Suggested Activities

1. List problems of your students' neighborhood on the board. Discuss what students can do (who they should complain to or what organization can help). Develop codes about the problems for further lessons.
2. Bring in a community organizer to talk about neighborhoods.
3. Write a class petition to a city agency, or even to the school administration.
4. Discuss whether or not students' neighborhoods are "communities."

V. IMMIGRATION OVERVIEW

Language in Immigration unit presented in the following lesson plans, codes 1–8:

Vocabulary: mode of travel (1)
immigration papers and experience (throughout)
advertisement (2, 4)
rights (6, 7)
citizenship (8)

Language functions and structures:

use past tense (throughout)
express duration (1, 5) — How long did it take?
make statement (2) — He told me . . . .
express hope (4)
offer assistance (5) — May I help you?
express preference (4, 8) — What do you like better?
express obligation (6) — should
make apology (6) — I'm sorry, but I'm in a hurry.

Immigration means more than crossing a border. To ESL students, it means a lengthy and difficult process of leaving a home country for an uncertain life and new identity in the United States. Who is an immigrant—a person with permanent resident status? Someone here temporarily? Someone who may apply for permanent status? When do people feel they have truly changed their homeland? When they become citizens? When they have children here? Perhaps never?

The answers to these questions are not simple for many ESL students who are uncertain of their home, how to bring their families together, or where they want to live permanently. As people talk about these issues in the classroom, they can help one another and feel more settled in the U.S. *and* build English skills.

Immigration is a touchy subject. Current debate in the media centers on America's responsibility for absorbing the world's poor and refugee populations. Quotas, the drain on social services, whether illegals can or should be deported—these are topics that provoke heated argument.

The Statue of Liberty has symbolized America's outstretched arms for all oppressed peoples, yet immigration policy has never been consistently open. With the first Chinese Exclusionary Act of 1882, immigration laws have fluctuated between open entry and exclusion, depending on our need for labor or our fear of foreigners. The first quota system, adopted in 1921, caused the Southern and Eastern European immigration to drop sharply.

Immigration policy toward Mexican nationals demonstrates the U.S. ambivalence. Mexican labor began to work the farm fields in the 1920s, following Chinese (originally brought for mine and railroad work), Japanese, and other groups. During the Depression, many were deported. With World War II and the growth of agribusiness, the demand for Mexican labor increased rapidly. Congress responded with the 1942 Bracero Program which allowed labor contractors to bring Mexicans back and forth as the season required. The Bracero program ended in 1964, and people who had become dependent on six months' work in the U.S. could no longer migrate legally. Then they became illegals.

Today Mexicans and other Latin Americans enter the U.S. to seek work or to join their families. Many of those who come illegally could immigrate legally if not for the three-to-five-year backlog of paperwork at the Immigration and Naturalization Service (INS). Others don't choose to settle permanently but travel back and forth regularly. People living on the border may have one citizenship but feel an allegiance to two countries. Others of Hispanic origin trace their ancestry before the 1848 U.S. annexation of the Southwest. Though U.S. citizens, they often face as much harassment as if they were undocumented persons. Puerto Ricans who leave their island are also often treated as foreigners despite the fact that they are U.S. citizens.

This unit explores the difficulties that changing restrictions and attitudes create for ESL students immigrating and settling in the U.S. To begin, teachers can ask students to define what immigration means to them. The answer might change throughout the unit as students have the opportunity to express why they immigrated, how they felt about leaving home, what expectations they had for life here, and how they feel now. In comparing experiences and tracing their journeys on a map, they will learn how and why the United States was settled by immigrant groups. Teachers can also provide an historical overview or bring in a speaker to talk of the immigrant experience and the different experiences for first and second generation citizens.

The paperwork involved in immigration is a major difficulty for many ESL students, and the class can provide basic survival skills: how to fill out immigration papers for a relative, how to talk to INS officials, how to obtain necessary documents.

Citizenship is a topic which may provoke major discussions on people's feelings of belonging to one or two countries. The class can provide information on how to become a citizen or how to resolve visa problems. Discussing the pros and cons of citizenship might enable people to make a better decision on the value of U.S. citizenship. The unit concludes by affirming our multicultural society.

Special Note:

Immigration is a sensitive theme, and teachers should exercise caution in this unit. Students may have entered the U.S. illegally, and will drop the class if they fear teachers will ask directly about their status. Extra care must also be taken with refugees. Their experiences might be too recent and painful to address formally. On the other hand, lessons presented in a supportive and respectful manner can help them become more comfortable in their new situations.

The following information (as of 1980) might be helpful to the discussion: Current U.S. immigration law limits legal entry to 20,000 people per country annually. The Western Hemisphere has a limit of 120,000. The Eastern Hemisphere's limit is 170,000.

Mexicans: 10% of Mexico's population lives in the U.S. California's population is 20% Spanish surname (1980 census). An estimated 7 million legal Mexican-Americans or green-carders live in the Southwest, with an additional 5–10 million illegal aliens in the U.S.

Puerto Ricans: There are 2 million living in the continental U.S.

Cubans: Current estimates are up to 900,000 residents.

Indochinese: As of 1980, over 600,000 refugees have come from Vietnam, Cambodia, and Laos.

Caribbean: In the last two decades alone, close to one million West Indians have immigrated.

A 1975 Department of Labor study determined that only .5% of illegals receive welfare, whereas 77% pay social security and income tax through their paycheck withholdings.

1. Coming to the United States

Mr. Lee: Hello, are you new here?

Carlos: Yes, Elba, the children, and I just came from Guatemala.

Mr. Lee: How did you come?

Elba: We came by bus.

Mr. Lee: How long did it take you?

Elba: It took four long days.

Carlos: When did you come to the United States, Mr. Lee?

Mr. Lee: I came thirty years ago.

Elba: Thirty years? Did you come alone?

Mr. Lee: Yes, I left my wife and children in China.

Carlos: That's sad. Are they here now?

Mr. Lee: My wife is here. My sons are in China.

Elba: How did you come?

Mr. Lee: Oh, that's a long story.

Tools for Dialogue

1. Where did Carlos and Elba come from?
   How long did it take?
   How did they come?
   When did Mr. Lee come?
   Who did he leave in China?

2. How did Mr. Lee feel when he left?
   How did Carlos and Elba feel?
   How did they feel on the trip?

3. Where are you from?
   When did you come?
   How did you come?
   How long did it take you?
   Did you come alone or with family?
   Who did you leave in your home country?
   Where did you cross the border?
   Did you make stops on the trip?

Conversation and Writing Circle

How did you feel when you left?
Did you feel sad? Why?
Did you feel happy? Why?
How did you feel on the trip?

Did you feel excited? Why?
Did you feel scared? Why?
How did you feel at the border?
How did you feel when you arrived?

Practice

present	*past*	
come	came	
take	took	
leave	left	
feel	felt	
walk	walked	by bus
cross	crossed	by plane
travel	traveled	by boat
arrive	arrived	by car

How long did it take?
    It took four days.

How long did the trip take you?
    It took me _____.

    _____.
    _____.

I feel/felt   _____.
    _____.
    _____.

sad, happy, excited, scared, nervous

Suggested Activities

1. Ask students, "What is immigration, what does it mean to you?"
2. Use world map. Place stick pins where students used to live. Have them trace their routes. Place a pin where they arrived and attach a string between points.
3. List and discuss the cultures that make up the United States today.

2. Why Did You Come?

My name is Mario Castro. I left Mexico twenty (20) years ago. I didn't have any money. A labor contractor from the U.S. came to my village. He told me I could go north and work in the farm fields. He told me I would make a lot of money. He took me to Salinas, California with other Mexicans. I paid him money to come. I worked for the summer, but then there was no more work. I found work in a cannery.

Tools for Dialogue

1. When did Mario leave?
   Who told him to come?
   What's a labor contractor?
   Who did he come with?
   Did he pay money?
   What did he do in Salinas?
   How long did he work in the fields?
   Where did he find work after summer?
2. Why did he leave?
   What did he think of the U.S.?
   Did he make a lot of money?
3. Why did you come?
   Did you come with a labor contractor?
   How did you hear about the United States?
   Did friends tell you? Did you get a letter?
   Did you see advertisements or signs?
4. Who makes money in the United States?
   What companies advertise in your home country?
   What do their signs say?
   Why do they advertise?

Practice

come.
He *told me* I could   go north.
                     go shopping.

When did he come?
     He came 20 years ago.
When did you come?
     I came _____ years ago.
            _____ months ago.

Suggested Activities

1. List on board the foreign companies that have offices or factories in students' countries. Ask where they see the products and who buys them. Ask how much wages are in their countries and how much in the U.S. Ask why companies want to have branches in foreign countries.

2. Have students write advertisements they've seen on the board.

3. Ask what jobs immigrants have; map out places where many immigrants work.

3. A Refugee's Story

My name is Maysao Thao. I was born in Laos in 1957. I helped my parents take care of my brothers and sisters. In 1975, my family decided to flee the war. We walked to Thailand. It took a long time. We only walked in the forest. We did not have food to eat. At the border we swam across the river. We arrived at Camp Nongkhai. It was safe.

I fell in love with Ying Vang. He had worked with the American people in our country, so he could come to the United States. He came without me because we weren't married then. Then my sister married an American and went to the United States. After three years, she sponsored me. I married Ying Vang because we missed each other very much.

Tools for Dialogue

1. Where was Maysao Thao born?
   How did her family leave Laos?
   How long did it take?
   How long did she stay in the camp?
   Who sponsored her to come to the U.S.?
   Did she marry Ying Vang?

2. What's a refugee?
   Is a refugee the same as an immigrant?
   Is three years a long time to stay in a camp?

3. Why did you leave your country?
   How did you feel?
   What were you looking for in the U.S.?
   Are you a refugee?
   Do you know refugees?

4. Why are there refugees?
   Why did Maysao's family leave Laos?
   What countries do refugees come from?
   Who can come to the United States?

5. How does the United States help refugees?
   How can the United States help refugees more?
   Who sponsored you?
   Can you sponsor others?

Practice

	went		a long time.
	quit		a short time.
I	swam	It took	a few days.
	arrived		a week.
	married		a month.

I *was* born   You *were* born
He/She was born   We were born
                 They were born

Suggested Activities

1. List on the board different refugee and immigrant groups that come to the United States. Discuss why different people come. Look at the U.S. as a multicultural society; discuss how groups are treated.
2. Bring in the U.N. Charter on Human Rights.

4. My Hopes About the United States

Mariana: Hello, Guillermo. How's life?

Guillermo: Oh, not so good.

Mariana: Why? What's wrong?

Guillermo: Oh, it's hard to make money here.

Felicia: I told you. One year is too short to make money.

Guillermo: In Cuba, the radio from Miami said it was easy.

Mariana: Easy? I've lived here for five years and I think it's hard.

Felicia: Can you hear American radio in Cuba?

Guillermo: Sure, all the time. They advertise everything.

Mariana: So what's wrong today?

Guillermo: Well, I went to the doctor and paid a lot of money. In Cuba doctors are free.

Felicia: Do you want to go back?

Guillermo: Sometimes, I miss my family. But I'm here now.

Tools for Dialogue

1. What's wrong with Guillermo?
   What does Miami radio say about the U.S.?
   What does the radio advertise?
   Where did Guillermo go today?
   Does Guillermo want to go back?

2. Did Guillermo hope to make money?
   Is it easy to make money here?

3. Before you came, what did you hope for?
   What did you want in the United States?
   Did you find what you wanted? Tell us.
   Was it easy or hard to find work?
   Was it easy or hard to find an apartment?
   Was it easy or hard to move?
   Who did you know here before you came?
   Who do you know now?

4. Why is it hard to move?
   Why is it hard to make money?
   Why do radios say it's easy?

5. Who helped you come to the United States?
   Do you want to stay here?
   Can you visit home?
   What do you like better about your home country?
   What do you like better about the United States?

A letter home

Dear Family,
   I'm living in a 2-room apartment on 103rd and First Avenue.
   There are five of us, my aunt, uncle, and two cousins. I have a job cleaning buildings after everyone goes home. On Saturdays we go out dancing. I like New York.
   It's cold here, not like Cuba. How is Juana's new kid? Well, got to go. I miss you.
                              Love,
                              Guillermo

Suggested Activities

1. Have students describe their old neighborhoods in their home country. Ask, "Where were you born? What did you like? What didn't you like? Who did you live with?"

2. Have students describe their lives in their home country. "When you were young, what did you do? What work did you do? What did you like better there?"

3. Have students tell what they like about the U.S.

4. Have students write a letter to family back home.

5. Immigration Papers

Secretary: Good morning, INS office. May I help you?

Mr. Godoy: Hello, I'd like information about bringing my wife to America.

Secretary: Are you a citizen?

Mr. Godoy: No, I'm a permanent resident. I have a green card.

Secretary: Where's your wife?

Mr. Godoy: She's in Guatemala.

Secretary: You need to fill out an I-130 form.

Mr. Godoy: Can you send it to me?

Secretary: Yes, I can. You also need proof of marriage.

Mr. Godoy: We married in Guatemala.

Secretary: That's okay. You also need proof you can support her.

Mr. Godoy: Okay. How long does it take to get a visa?

Secretary: Oh, it takes a long time—sometimes four or five years.

Tools for Dialogue

1. Where is Mr. Godoy calling?
   Is he a citizen?
   What does he ask the secretary?
   Where's his wife?

2. What papers does he need? What does he need to prove?
   How long does it take to get a visa?
   Is it easy to bring family to the U.S.?

3. What papers did you need?
   Did you have a sponsor? Who?
   Was it hard to get the visa?
   Did you use a lawyer?
   How long did you wait?

4. How do you get a green card?
   How much money do you need?
   How long does it take? Why?

5. Who can help you bring someone to the U.S.?
   Who can help you get papers?
   Do you think it should take so long?

Practice

How long does it take to . . . ?
It takes a long time.
   2 years

How long does it take to come by bus?
                      by plane?
                      by boat?
                      by walking?

Suggested Activities

1. Bring in copies of forms to fill out for practice.
2. List on board who you can sponsor and who you can't. Bring in copies of the immigration laws.
3. Have someone from an Institute or voluntary agency that helps people immigrate come in and speak to the class.
4. Have students roleplay interviews with INS officials, border patrol, customs at airport, lawyers, and officials in agencies that can help students. Dialogues can cover refugees who are sponsoring family from the camps (this requires knowing who is allowed and who isn't), and people going through the normal INS procedures.
5. Create a written dialogue for refugees filling out necessary papers.

6. Border Problems

Border Patrol: Hey, you! Why are you running through here?

Sr. Garcia: I have to catch a bus. It leaves for L.A. in 15 minutes.

Border Patrol: This is a government area. You can't run through here.

Sr. Garcia: I'm sorry, but I'm late.

Border Patrol: May I see your papers, please?

Sr. Garcia: I'm a U.S. citizen. I don't need papers.

Border Patrol: Then may I see your driver's license?

Sr. Garcia: I don't drive.

Border Patrol: How about your birth certificate?

Sr. Garcia: Listen, I'm on the U.S. side of the border.

Border Patrol: Well, how do I know you're not an illegal immigrant?

Sr. Garcia: I know my rights.

Border Patrol: All right. All right. But you should carry papers.

Tools for Dialogue

1. Why is Sr. Garcia running?
   What does the patrolman ask?
   Does Sr. Garcia have papers with him?
   Does he have a driver's license?
   Where is Sr. Garcia?

2. Is Sr. Garcia a citizen?
   Does a citizen need papers?
   Why is the patrolman unfriendly?
   How does Sr. Garcia feel?

3. Are you a citizen?
   Do you carry papers?
   Has someone asked you for papers?
   Were they friendly or unfriendly?
   How did you feel?

4. Why is the patrolman asking for papers?
   Why do border guards try to stop undocumented people?

5. What can you say if someone asks for papers?
   What can you say if they are unfriendly?
   What are your rights?

Practice

You should	carry papers. walk through here. go home. get a license.

I'm sorry, but	I'm late. I'm busy. I'm in a hurry. I'm not feeling well. I can't stay. I can't help you. . . .

Suggested Activities

1. Call local immigration office or legal services to find out rights of permanent residents and illegal immigrants. Bring in information and discuss.
2. Bring in information on illegals. Discuss jobs they have, the fact that they seldom take away jobs from U.S. citizens, the special problems their children face, etc.

7. My Rights

(Abstracted from the American Civil Liberties Union advice card,
YOU AND THE POLICE)

If You Are Stopped By The Police:

1. You must identify yourself. Give your name and address. Show a good identification card, driver's license or car registration card if you are driving.

2. Ask if you are under arrest. You have the right to know.

3. You don't have to talk with the police. You don't have to answer questions if you don't want to.

4. If you decide to talk, anything you say can be used against you.

5. The police may "pat-down" your clothing or search your car if they think you have weapons. You don't have to agree to the search. Tell the police if you don't agree.

6. If you are arrested, you have the right to a lawyer immediately. You can have a lawyer with you while the police ask you questions.

7. If you don't have money, you can have a lawyer for free.

8. If you are arrested, you have the right to two free phone calls within three hours after the arrest.

Suggested Activities

1. These are not complete rights of someone arrested, but basic rights that everyone should know. Write these on a transparency and go over the meaning with the students. Ask, "What are your rights?" The ACLU distributes wallet cards in three languages that contain these rights. They will send a classroom set for distribution.

2. Develop dialogues about encounters with the police. Try to be as realistic as possible by asking students if they've ever been stopped or questioned by the police.

3. Discuss the need for police—when they are helpful, when they are not helpful.

4. Have a police officer come to class to talk about his or her duties and to listen to students' opinions about the police in their communities.

8. I'm a Citizen

>   Son: Hey, it's your eighteenth birthday. You can register to vote.
> Daughter: I know. I'm excited. Father, don't you want to vote?
>   Father: I'm a Japanese citizen.
>   Son: You're Japanese, but we're American citizens.
>   Father: Yes, you are Japanese-Americans. You were born here.
> Daughter: And you've lived in the U.S. for 19 years.
>   Father: Japan is my home.
>   Son: You don't live there anymore.
>   Father: I go back and visit my family. I like the people better there. I have two homes.
> Daughter: Yes, I like people in Japan too, but America is my home.

Tools for Dialogue

1. Who can register to vote? Why?
   Where is the father a citizen?
   Can he vote there?
   Where are the son and daughter citizens?
   How long has the father lived in the United States?
   Does the father visit Japan?
2. Where does father feel at home?
   What does he like about Japan?
   What does he like about the U.S.?
   Where are his children at home?
3. Where are you a citizen?
   How long have you lived in the U.S.?
   Where do you feel at home?
4. Do you want to be a U.S. citizen? Why? Why not?
   Do you vote?
   Is voting important?
5. What are your rights as a permanent resident?
   What are your rights as a citizen?
   How can you be a citizen?
   What do you need to know?

Practice

Where are you from?

	Mexico.	I'm a Mexican citizen.
	Jamaica.	Jamaican
I'm from	Nicaragua.	Nicaraguan
	Russia.	Russian
	China.	Chinese
	Vietnam.	Vietnamese . . .
		I'm an American citizen.

Suggested Activities

1. List on the board the *students'* views on the pros and cons of being U.S. citizens.
2. During political elections, review campaign literature and issues in class.
3. Take a tour to City Hall or another government office.
4. Bring in citizenship test, application forms and any government publications.
5. Bring in bilingual copies of the Treaty of Guadalupe Hidalgo, 1848, that provides the history of the Southwest as a bilingual/bicultural area (if class is Spanish-speaking).
6. Discuss the existence of Japanese internment camps during World War II.

VI. HEALTH OVERVIEW

Language in Health unit presented in following lesson plans, codes 1–8:

Vocabulary: describing symptoms and what's wrong to doctors (1)
taking medicines (2)
medical insurance (3)
workers' compensation (5)
filling out medical forms (6)
stress (7)
describing good health (8)

Language functions and structures:

use present perfect tense (throughout)
express frequency (1, 5, 8) — always, often, sometimes, never,
a lot, a little
give advice (2) — should
state opinion (3) — I think _____ .
ask for explanation (3) — Why don't _____ ?
state emphasis (7) — It must be _____ .
use the word "get" to mean acquire (5) — Get a doctor.
use the word "get" to mean become (8) — Get sick, get tired.

The concern for health reaches into every area of life. When people feel good, they take their physical and mental health for granted. They eat what they feel like eating, go to work, sleep as many hours as they have time for, and visit a doctor occasionally for a checkup. Many people only use the doctor for physicals required in a job application, for children's regular visits, for gynecological services (women), and for emergencies. People's health, therefore, depends more on their lifestyle (how much they smoke, drink, exercise) and environment (particularly work situations) than on the use of medical care services.

This unit on health integrates the three areas: 1) use of the medical system; 2) personal health habits; and 3) the conditions in neighborhoods and workplaces that promote ill health.

Many ESL students are mainly concerned with the first area—how to negotiate the medical care system. New immigrants, refugees, and non-English-speaking U.S. citizens are not likely to use regular preventative services or to be in healthful living and work environments. ESL students, often low-income and uninsured, rely heavily on emergency rooms and on county clinics; they don't have private physicians who know their medical histories.

Getting good health care is often problematic. Non-English speakers often have difficulty communicating their symptoms and needs to the doctor or nurse. They find bureaucratic procedures overly complicated. An even greater problem involves cultural mores that inhibit the seeking of preventative service. Latina women, for example, often do not have regular gynecological exams because they don't want to undress before male doctors.

This unit incorporates survival skills required for obtaining routine medical care. The dialogues encourage students to talk about their communication problems and what they've done to overcome them. This may give people confidence to try to make the system work *for* them. Specific topics include what to do in an emergency, how to make an appointment, how to fill out medical forms, how to describe symptoms, and how to get prescriptions filled. Health insurance (and how to analyze what it covers) is also discussed.

Throughout the unit, special attention is paid to students' cultures and values. Often students have a reservoir of cultural or folk health practices that can be useful in teaching other students. Many people from other countries maintain healthier eating habits than the average American. They eat more grains, beans, vegetables, and fruit, which the American diet has supplanted with processed foods high in sugars, fats, and cholesterol. Students can be encouraged to share their information while examining healthy and unhealthy practices in the U.S.

1. Calling the Clinic

Receptionist: County Clinic. May I help you?

Felicia: My son is very sick. His head hurts. It's hot.

Receptionist: What? Oh, you mean he has a fever. What's his name?

Felicia: His name is Pablo Ramirez. R-A-M-I-R-E-Z.

Receptionist: Has he been here before?

Felicia: Excuse me, can you repeat that please?

Receptionist: That's OK. I'll check his record.

Receptionist: We don't have a record for Pablo Ramirez. He needs to come in to the clinic.

Felicia: Can you speak slower, please?

Receptionist: He needs to come in.

Felicia: Can he see the doctor?

Receptionist: Yes, bring him after one o'clock. The clinic opens at one.

Felicia: When?

Receptionist: (loudly) After one o'clock tomorrow.

Felicia: Oh, one o'clock. Does anyone speak Spanish there?

Receptionist: No, I'm sorry.

Tools for Dialogue

1. Where is Felicia calling?
   What's the matter with Pablo?
   Does the clinic have a record for Pablo?
   When does the clinic open?

2. Does Felicia have an appointment?
   Is that a problem?
   Does anyone speak Spanish there?
   Does Felicia understand?
   Is the receptionist impolite? Why?

3. How does the story make you feel?
   Do you have a neighborhood clinic?
   Do you have to wait? Are there long lines?
   Does anyone speak your language there?

4. Do they need bilingual speakers at the clinic?
   Is it important for doctors and nurses to understand you?
   Why are there lines at the clinic?

5. What can you do when you don't understand?
   What can the clinic do when people don't speak English?
   What can the clinic do when there are long lines?

Conversation Circle

How do you feel?	I feel	sick/tired.		S(he) feels sick/tired.
What's the matter?		a cold.		She has a fever/sore throat.
	I have	a fever.		
		a headache.	My head	hurts a lot.
		a stomachache.	stomach	hurts a little.
	She has	a backache.	Her back	hurts all the time.
		a toothache.	His tooth	hurts.
			His leg	hurts.

Suggested Activities

1. Teach body parts through total physical response, figure drawings, games like Simon Says.
2. Have students role-play parents calling a clinic to make an appointment, calling work to say they have to stay home with a sick child, calling the school to say the child is out sick.
3. Divide students in pairs; one is sick, one is the doctor. Have them practice describing what's wrong with them.
4. Have students write a letter to a child's teacher or school dean explaining why the child was out sick. Include symptoms, notice of doctor's visit, apologies.

2. At the Drugstore

Hung: Excuse me. I have a bad cold and a terrible cough. What can I take?

Druggist: We have cough medicine. Have you seen a doctor?

Hung: No, no. I just want a bottle of cough medicine.

Druggist: OK, here's a good one.

Hung: Ten dollars! Wow! Do you have a cheaper medicine?

Druggist: Yes, I do. This one is for the same problem, but it's not a brand name. It's six dollars.

Hung: That's fine. What are the instructions?

Druggist: Take one teaspoon every six hours. It's on the label. You should take a teaspoon at bedtime.

Tools for Dialogue

1. What does Hung have?
   Has he seen a doctor?
   What does the druggist give him?
   Does he ask for a cheaper medicine?

2. Why is it cheaper?
   What's a brand name drug?
   Why does the druggist want to sell brand names?
   Does Hung know what he's taking?

3. What do you buy at a drugstore?
   Do you buy over-the-counter drugs?
   Do you buy prescription drugs?
   In your home country, what do you buy at a drugstore?
   Do you need prescriptions to buy drugs? Are prescriptions good?
   In your country, what do you do for a cold? A fever? A headache? A sore throat? A stomachache?
   Do you use herbs?
   What is better about the U.S.? about your country?

4. In the U.S., why are brand name drugs more expensive?
   Why do people take a lot of drugs?

5. Can you ask for cheaper medicines?
   Should druggists sell you cheap medicines?
   Should druggists take Med-i-caid?
   How can you stay healthy?

Practice

You are sick. What should you do?
You have a cold.
You have a cough. What should you do?

    Should you go to a doctor?
    Should you take aspirin?
    Should you stay home from work?
    Should you drink juices?
    Should you take cough medicine?

      I should _____.

Suggested Activities

1. Bring in different medicines and read directions. Vocabulary: (*teaspoon, pill, tablet, take daily, every two hours*) Mini-dialogues:

    How many pills should I take? Read the label.
            teaspoons   You should take one every day.
                          You should take one every four hours.

2. Have students role-play asking the druggist for something for a stomach-ache, asking if the drugstore accepts Med-i-caid or other insurance.

3. Read the labels of many different over-the-counter and prescription drugs. Ask, "What are the dosages? What are the cautions? What happens if you don't follow directions?"

    Examples: Mrs. F. Garcia   Bayer Aspirin
                 Take as directed   Adults: 1 or 2 tablets
                 24 Cortisone, 5 mg.   with water—
                 Do not use after Jan. 81   not more than
                                             8 daily
                                    Caution: If pains persist,
                                             be sure to con-
                                           sult a physi-
                                           cian.
                             Keep away from children.

4. If students have questions about drugs or problems such as mislabeling that you can't answer, the Federal Drug Administration has a toll-free hotline for reporting such problems (800) 638-6725.

3. How Do You Pay?

Ambulance Driver: What happened? Where's the victim?
  Paul: Here, on the ground.
Driver: What's his name, address, and phone number?
  Paul: His name is Mark Wong. He is my brother. We live at 14 Jackson Street. Our phone number is 524-1134.
Driver: It looks like a broken arm. Where does it hurt?
  Mark: My arm hurts. My back hurts here.
Driver: Does he have insurance?
  Paul: He has Med-i-caid.
Driver: Where's the card?
  Paul: I think it's at home.
Driver: Then I have to take him to the County Hospital.
  Paul: But that's far away. There's a private hospital right down the street.
Driver: I'm sorry. I have to.

Tools for Dialogue

1. What's the matter with Mark Wong?
   Does he have health insurance?
   Where's his card?
   Where is the driver taking Mark? Is it far?

2. How does Mark feel?
   Does he need emergency care?
   Why doesn't the driver take him to the private hospital?
   Does the driver have a choice?

3. Do you have health insurance?
   How do you pay for doctors?
   Do you carry your card?
   Are you eligible for Med-i-caid?

4. Why don't some doctors take Med-i-caid?
   Why don't private hospitals take patients without insurance?
   Why doesn't insurance cover everything?

5. Do you think doctors should take Med-i-caid?
   How do you get Med-i-caid? Where do you go?
   Which hospitals take patients without insurance?

Emergency Mini-Dialogue

      Paul: This is an emergency. I'll call an ambulance.

Operator: Your name and the number you are calling from, please.

      Paul: Paul Wong, 524-1134.

Operator: What's the emergency?

      Paul: It looks like he broke his arm.   /fell from the ladder.

                         had an accident.   /had a heart attack.

                         burned his leg.

Practice

I think it's at home.

            it's a broken arm.

            he's hurt.

            he's upset.

            he's okay.

Suggested Activities

1. Have students roleplay calling an ambulance and telling where the accident is, telling the driver or police what happened.

2. Let them bring in their phone books to look up emergency numbers, hospitals, neighborhood clinics, and other community services. Develop an emergency card including: police dept., fire dept., ambulance, emergency room at nearest hospital, family doctor, poison control center, bus information. Discuss why people need these numbers and when they should call them.

3. Develop exercises from the first section of the phone book which has first aid information, emergency numbers, dialing instructions and local area information. Have students make calls for information and report back to class.

4. Go over student's insurance. Ask, "What does it cover? Who pays for it?"

4. Neighborhood Health

Tools for Dialogue

1. What is in the picture?
   Who is on the street?
   Does the street light work?
   What time is it?

2. Is this neighborhood safe? Why or why not?
   Where does the dog come from?
   Why is the child frightened?
   What can happen next?

3. What are the health problems in your neighborhood?
   Do you have stray dogs? rats?
   Do you have broken glass? problems with garbage?
   What kinds of accidents are there in your neighborhood?
   Is there an emergency room or clinic near you?
   Is your neighborhood safe?
   Can you walk alone at night?

4. Why do you think your neighborhood is safe? not safe?
   Why are there stray dogs?
   Where can you get good medical care in your neighborhood?

5. What can you do about the glass? the dogs? the garbage?
   What would you like to change in your neighborhood?
   Do you know your neighbors?
   Is there a neighborhood organization?
   Is there a place where everyone gets together?

Suggested Activity

1. Read and discuss the following story.

Dog bites are a health problem in many neighborhoods. In Chicago, one neighborhood organization discovered many people came to the emergency room because of dog bites. Wild dogs frightened the neighborhood children. The organization decided to offer $5.00 to anyone who captured stray dogs and turned them in. After one month, 160 dogs were captured and there were fewer dog bites.

5. Work Health

Nurse: Reza Kashmir please. Come into the doctor's office.

Taghi: Can I come too? Reza doesn't speak much English.

Nurse: Sure.

Doctor: Okay. What's the matter? Who's the patient here?

Taghi: He is.

Doctor: Where's his record? What's your problem?

Reza: My back hurts.

Taghi: He pulled a muscle last week at work. He was lifting a very heavy box and felt a sharp pain.

Doctor: Have you hurt your back before?

Taghi: Yes, he often hurts his back at work.

Doctor: It's only a pulled muscle. Here's a prescription for the pain. Go home and rest for a few days.

Reza: What about work?

Doctor: Can't you get workers' compensation?

Tools for Dialogue

1. Does Reza speak English?
   What's his problem?
   What was Reza doing at work?
   Has he hurt his back before?

2. What does the doctor give him for the pain?
   What does the doctor tell him to do?
   Can Reza rest for a few days?
   Will he get paid? Will he get workers' compensation?

3. Have you ever hurt yourself at work?
   Do people have back problems at your work?
   What are the health problems at your work?
      Do you work with chemicals?
      Do you work with a torch?
   How does your work make you feel?

4. Why do you think there are health problems at work?
   Do you wear gloves, boots, goggles, or any special clothes?
   How can you protect yourself?

5. How can you get workers' compensation? How can you get disability?
   Is it easy to get? Do you know anyone who got workers' compensation?
   Do you want more information?

Practice—to get (to acquire)

Can't you *get* workers' compensation?
      I get disability.
     She gets her pay check.
    He gets good money at his job.

	hurt your back?	Yes, I have.
	pulled a muscle?	No, I haven't.
	burned a finger?	No, I've never . . .
	cut your hand?	Yes, I've often . . . .
Have you ever	broken your arm?	
	felt sick?	
	had a fever?	
	had a headache?	
	had a sore throat?	
	had a cold?	

6. Medical Role-Plays

MEDICAL HISTORY FORM

Name _____ Date _____

      last   first

Address _____ Phone _____

Birthdate _____ Weight _____ Height _____

Insurance Company _____ Policy Number _____

If you don't have insurance, who should be billed? _____

Place a check next to any problems you have had:

_____ Allergies
_____ Diabetes
_____ Skin rash
_____ Stomach upset
_____ Frequent colds
_____ Bad headaches
_____ High blood pressure
_____ Heart attacks
_____ Asthma

Surgeries _____ Dates _____

              _____   _____

Medications you _____ Allergies to _____
   are taking   medications

Have students work in pairs to fill out the medical history form. One student will be the health care provider and ask questions to get the information; the other will be the patient. Switch roles.

Suggested Activities

1. Have students role-play the following situations.
   a) Discuss with a doctor a problem you have from work. Did it only happen once or is it a problem that recurs?
   b) Register at an emergency room after a car accident, back injury, oven burn, etc. Be the patient, accompanying friend and receptionist. Fill out appropriate forms.
   c) Use phone book to look up doctors for specific problems or needs: pediatricians, optometrists, dentists, etc. Ask how you find good doctors.
   d) Bring your child to the dentist to have her teeth cleaned, cavities filled, cap placed over chipped tooth, or just a regular checkup.

2. Role-play class situations: Someone in class gets a nosebleed. What do you do?
   Someone in class sprains his ankle. What do you do?
   Someone in class has a headache. What do you do?

3. Develop exercises on disaster situations: an earthquake, a flood, a hurricane, a tornado, a fire in the school building, a blackout.

7. Stress at Work—Honju Na's Story

I work in a garment factory. It is so hot there, especially in the summer. Then it must be over 100 degrees. There's only one fan on the ceiling, and you can't feel it.

I'm a strong woman, but I'm exhausted at the end of the day. I stand all day pressing clothes. My back aches. My legs ache, and work never stops. I feel so tense there.

People go crazy. They take aspirins or tranquilizers. Sometimes I take valium.

Tools for Dialogue

1. Where does Honju work?
   How does she feel at the end of the day?
   How do her muscles feel?
   Why is it hot?

2. Is Honju's work making her sick?
   Why does her work never stop?
   How long can she keep working there?
   Can she get a better job?

3. How do you feel at work? At the end of the day?
   Do you feel tense?
   Do you feel nervous?
   How does your body feel when you are tense?

4. What do people take at work to help them?
   Why do people take aspirin or valium?
   Why doesn't she have protections at work?

5. Are aspirins or valium good for you? What do they do?
   What would make your work better?
   Do you have a union?
   Can you get a better job?

Practice

It's so hot.		over 100 degrees.
It's so cold.		less than 5°.
I'm so tired.	It must be	midnight.
I'm so hungry.		lunchtime.
		time to punch out.
		the end of the day.

Suggested Activities

1. Make a list on board of what creates stress at work: kind of work (have students describe fully), length of work hours, working at night, pace of work, not being able to talk to co-workers.
   Discuss if students feel tense all the time or just sometimes. Discuss what they can or can't do.

2. Discuss with students how they feel under stress. Do their muscles tense or ache? Do they get headaches? Feel nervous, angry or upset?

3. Ask what students do when they feel stress:
   "What's good for you?
   What's bad for you?"

   "Do you take aspirins?
   Do you drink coffee?
   Do you drink alcohol?
   Do you take valium?
   Do you stay home and rest?
   Do you talk to someone?
   Do you relax? How do you relax?
   Do you change your job? Can you?"

8. My Health

Tools for Dialogue

1. What is the mother making?
   What is she eating?
   What is she saying?

2. Who is she making breakfast for?
   Is she going to eat breakfast?
   Is breakfast important for health?
   What is she doing that's unhealthy?
   Why is she in a hurry? Does she feel stress?

3. What do you eat that's healthy? that's unhealthy?
   What do you do that's unhealthy?
   When do you feel stress?
   When do you get sick?

4. Do you get sick when you don't eat well?
   Do you get sick when you work hard?
   Does anything in your job make you sick?
   Do you have time to get sick?

5. How can you eat well?
   Can you change anything in your job?
   Can you relax outside your job?
   Can other people help you at home?
   What do you do to stay healthy?
     Do you eat well?
     Do you exercise?
     Do you spend time with friends?
     Do you sleep well?
     Do you relax?

Conversation Circle and Writing Exercise

> get sick?
> get tired?
When do you get nervous?
> get headaches?
> get a cold or fever?

> always
> often
Do you get sick often? Yes, I sometimes get sick.
> seldom
> never

What can you do about that?

Suggested Activities

1. Make a list of things in students' lives that make them feel tense or feel stress (going for a job interview, speaking English to the doctor, having to feed many children, being unemployed).
   What do they do when they feel stress? — Have students share ideas.
   > What can they do that's healthy? What can they do to relax?
   > What can they do to change the situation?

2. Introduce relaxation exercises into classrooms. There are many to choose from: simple visualizations, tension/relaxation of muscles, massage. Have someone from a clinic or center teach exercises or call a center for prior instruction.

3. Bring in a public health nurse to talk about nutrition. Ask nurse to keep in mind culturally appropriate diets.

4. Have students bring in food labels. Discuss additives, preservatives, extra salt, sugar.

VII. WORK OVERVIEW

Language in Work unit presented in following lesson plans, codes 1-8:

Vocabulary: describing jobs (2)
    housework (3)
    applying for work (3, 4)
    unemployment (5)
    feelings about job interviews (5)
    women's work (7)
    health and safety (8)
    union (9)

Language functions and structures:

    request information (1) — Can you get a license?
    express obligation (2) — have to
    use present perfect tense (3)
    make comparison (6) — She wants a better job.
    express future intention (7) — I'll call you.
    express pain (8) — It hurts.
    make suggestion (7) — Maybe you should _____.

  Work is central to our lives. Work, or the lack of it, determines and shapes our position in society, our self-image and our physical and mental health. Because work occupies so much of our time, it has been said in the U.S., that we live to work. The U.S. work-day normally lasts from 8:30 to 5:00 with a half-hour lunch break. In other areas of the world, attitudes toward work are considerably different. In Latin cultures many workers still go home to their families for a two-hour lunch and siesta. In much of rural Indochina, work is part of daily life. The family toils long hours to produce their food, clothing, and shelter, but promptness and the time clock do not exist as cultural values.

  This unit starts by asking students to describe what work means to them: what are their jobs and job duties, in and outside the home. A lesson plan on "hands" can elicit a new look at work: Everyday tasks that people do with their hands, such as stirring a pot of food, become more important as students realize they "work" and "make culture" each day.

  A spectrum of important work issues are explored: work as social status; the difference between "women's work" and "men's work"; cultural differences in work attitudes; the availability of work; unemployment; the causes of differing working conditions, pay scales, hours, health and safety problems; and the role of unions. Survival skills teach how to complete job application forms, perform well in interviews, look for work, and compete for better jobs.

The majority of ESL students enter the U.S. job market in manual jobs or unskilled positions. Many work in nonunionized workplaces. New immigrants and minorities have traditionally filled low status jobs that Anglo-Americans or less recent immigrants won't take. As a consequence, many ESL students feel humiliated that they can't work at their previous skill level or that they can't achieve a higher position in America. One student who drove trucks, commented, "My work? Sure, it's hard, but it's not important." People often internalize their lack of job status, thinking it's their fault because they don't know English.

These feelings of self-blame reflect the conflicts of learning English. Students feel pressured to learn English for jobs they still might not get. Women experience discrimination in jobs or promotions. Students encounter lay-offs in industry, seasonal unemployment in the fields and canneries, discrimination in hiring practices, and lack of union protection.

Another issue is the type of work that women and men do and can do. Accepted employment for women in many parts of the world—driving tractors, carrying heavy loads, working as machinists—is considered nontraditional in America. This unit encourages women to discuss what they want in work outside the home, and relate these goals to work *in* the home. Do they experience a double workload? What if they didn't do housework? Are there alternatives, such as shared housework or childcare? During this unit, teachers can help create an environment where students can overcome feelings of inadequacy or individual failure and focus on what is important and necessary about their work and future aspirations. Ultimately these discussions could provide the framework for real change to improve our students' lives.

1. What Is Your Job?

Yuri: Hello, Natasha. This is Tony. He works at Sears.
Natasha: Oh, what do you do?
Tony: I'm a student.
Natasha: No, what do you do for a living?
Tony: What?
Yuri: She means, what is your job?
Tony: Oh, I'm a salesclerk. What do you do?
Natasha: I'm a salesclerk too, but I was a nurse in Russia.
Tony: Do you want to be a nurse here?
Natasha: Yes, but I need to get a U.S. license.
Yuri: Can you get one?
Natasha: I don't know.

Tools for Dialogue

1. What does Tony do for a living?
   Where does he work?
   What does Natasha do?
   What did she do in Russia?

2. Does Natasha like her job?
   Does Natasha want to be a nurse here?
   Why can't she be a nurse here now?
   Does she have skills?
   How can she get a license?

3. What do you do for a living?
   Where do you work?
   What did you do in your home country?
   Can you do that work here? Why or why not?
   What work do you want to do here? Can you?

4. Is your work hard or easy?
   Is your work important or necessary for society?

Practice

What do you do?
What do you do for a living?
What's your job?
What's your occupation?

Can you
get a license?
get a job?
get good grades?
get unemployment?

Suggested Activities

1. Ask students what work means to them.
2. List students' jobs on the board. Ask, "What do you do?" (Include house-work as a job.) Ask about family members as well.
   What hours do you work?
   Do you work full-time or part-time?
   Do you ever work overtime? Do you have to?
   What skills do you have?
   What tools do you use?
   Is your work hard?
   Is your work important? How do you feel about your job?
   What do you like about your job?
   What don't you like about your job?
   What would you like to change?
3. Bring in pictures of people at work. Have students describe jobs to build vocabulary: *he's cutting wheat, he's welding, she's sorting* . . . .
4. Design job category exercises: I build houses, I'm a _____.
   I drive trucks, I'm a _____.
   I take care of sick people, I'm a _____.

2. Work in the Home

Sharon Liu: Hello, Fatima. What are you doing?
    Fatima: I'm cleaning the house. How was your day?
Lonnie Yu: Oh, the same tiring job.
    Fatima: I'm tired, too. Cleaning is hard work.
    Sharon: I know. I have to clean my apartment when I get home.
    Lonnie: Oh, come over first for a cup of coffee.
    Sharon: Okay. I have to wait for my husband anyway.
    Fatima: Why do you have to wait?
    Sharon: I can't move the sofa. It's too heavy.
    Lonnie: Sure you can, if we help you.

Tools for Dialogue

1. What is Fatima doing?
   Is Fatima tired?
   Does Sharon have to clean her apartment?
2. Why does Sharon have to wait?
   Is she strong?
   Can she do hard work?
   How many hours does Sharon work? At her job? At home?
3. Do you work outside your home?
   Do you work inside your home?
   Do you want to work outside?
   Do you want to work inside?
   How many hours do you work?
   How do you feel at the end of the day?
   Are you tired after housework?
4. Is housework hard work?
   Can women do hard work?
   Do you get paid for housework?
   Do men work in the house?
5. Do you think women should work at home?
   Do you think men should work at home?

Practice

<table>
<tr><td rowspan="8">I have to</td><td>do housework.</td></tr>
<tr><td>clean the house.</td></tr>
<tr><td>cook dinner.</td></tr>
<tr><td>sweep the bedroom.</td></tr>
<tr><td>mop floors.</td></tr>
<tr><td>dry dishes.</td></tr>
<tr><td>wash clothes.</td></tr>
<tr><td>dust the shelf.</td></tr>
</table>

Suggested Activities

1. Describe housework. Have students write what they do in the house.

2. Bring pictures of women doing all kinds of work in different countries: farm work, nontraditional work in trades, housework, etc.

      Is it hard?   Is it important?

3. Develop exercises on HANDS to teach vocabulary and to have students reexamine the tasks which they take for granted.

   Have students fill in orally: I use my hands to _____

   write, make tortillas, eat, clap, pack tomatoes, sweep . . .

   Make a COLLAGE OF HANDS. Ask: What are hands doing, are they a man's or a woman's hands, what work do they do, is it hard work, are they young or old hands, left or right . . . ?

   Vary exercise: I work with both hands.

   My hand shake is strong/weak. Raise your right/left hand . . .

3. Looking for Work

Anita: Hello, Mario. How are you?

Mario: I'm nervous. I have a job interview in two hours.

Anita: Is this your first interview?

Mario: Yes, and I need a job. It's a truck driver's job at a warehouse.

Anita: You'll do okay. Dress neatly and be friendly.

Mr. Blake: Good morning, Mr. Duran. Have you filled out the form?

Mario Duran: Yes, I have. Here it is.

Mr. Blake: Have you driven a truck before?

Mario Duran: Yes, I have driven a pickup. I used to live on a farm.

Mr. Blake: Have you had experience in the United States?

Mario Duran: No, this is my first job interview.

Mr. Blake: Do you have letters of recommendation?

Mario Duran: No, but I think I can get them.

Mr. Blake: This is a permanent job. Are you planning to stay here?

Mario Duran: Yes, I want a permanent job.

Mr. Blake: Okay, can you work overtime or on Saturdays?

Mario Duran: Sometimes, but I have a family.

Mr. Blake: Thank you, Mr. Duran. I'll call you in a few days.

Mario Duran: Excuse me. Can you tell me the pay?

Tools for Dialogue

1. Why is Mario nervous?
   What's the job?
   Has Mario driven a truck before?
   Has he had experience in the U.S.?
   Does he have letters of recommendation?
   Can he work overtime?

2. How does Mario feel in the interview?
   Does Mario get the job?
   Is Mr. Blake friendly?
   Does he allow Mario to ask questions?

3. Do you have a job? Have you worked before?
   How did you find the job?
   How do you feel looking for work?
   How do you feel in the job interview?

4. Is it hard to get work? Why?
   What do you need to get work? experience? references?
   What helps in the job interview? How can you be less nervous?

5. Can you ask questions in the interview?
   What can you ask?
   What questions can your employer ask?
   Do you have to answer every question?

Practice—present perfect

I have	filled out	
You have	driven	. . . before.
He/She has	worked	. . . for a long time.
They have	lived	
We have	looked	. . . for two weeks.
	had experience	

Vocabulary

employer	employee
boss	worker
supervisor	
manager	

Suggested Activities

1. List on board how to find a job (ask friends/family, go to employment office, look in newspapers). Bring in want ads to decipher. Practice calling to set up appointments and role-playing interviews.

2. Teach students to fill out application forms and write resumes/letters to employers.

3. List on board what you can ask (or want to know) when you apply for job. List what employer can ask and what employer cannot ask.

4. Job Application

APPLICATION FORM: Fill out the form. Print neatly.

Last Name	First Name	Middle Initial	Height	Weight
Address (Number, Street)			Birthdate	
City	State	Zip Code	Phone Number	

EDUCATION AND TRAINING (circle highest grade completed) 1 2 3 4 5 6 7 8
high school 9 10 11 12
college 13 14 15 16

Name of Last School Attended	Years Attended	Major	Degree

PREVIOUS JOB EXPERIENCE (list three last jobs, use back of paper if necessary)

Name of Company	Your Title
Address of Company	Your Responsibilities
Supervisor	

Employed from to	Salary	Reason for Leaving
month year month year		

Have students work in pairs, one as the interviewer, one as the applicant. They can switch roles, fill out their own application, or their partner's application. After pair practice, they can demonstrate their dialogues for the rest of the class.

Interviewer: questions for the applicant:

1) What kind of work do you want?
2) Do you have work experience?
   Where have you worked?
   What was your last job?
   How long did you have your last job?
   What were your responsibilities?
   What was your salary?
   Why did you leave your last job?
3) What's your education?
   What's the highest grade you completed?
4) Do you have references?

Interviewee: questions for the employer:

1) Can you tell me more about the job?
   What kind of work is it?
   What are my responsibilities?
   Do I need special clothes?
2) What are the hours?
   Is there a lot of overtime?
   Is there weekend work?
3) What's the pay or salary?
   How much is overtime pay?
4) Are there possibilities for advancement?
   What would I have to do?

Other questions for the interview:

1) Do you have a car? Can you get here by bus?
2) Can you work on weekends?
3) Can you work overtime?
4) What salary do you want?

5. Laid Off

Narciso: Hi, Ricardo. What are you doing?

Ricardo: I'm looking for work. I was laid off five months ago.

Sabina: What do you do?

Ricardo: I'm a welder. I worked in an auto plant.

Narciso: How many people were laid off?

Ricardo: Oh, about 100 from the graveyard shift and 50 from swing shift.

Sabina: Do you get unemployment?

Ricardo: Of course. I have three children.

Narciso: That's good.

Ricardo: Yes, but my unemployment ends next week.

Tools for Dialogue

1. What is Ricardo doing?
   Why isn't he working?
   What does Ricardo do?
   Does he have children?

2. How many people were laid off?
   Does he get unemployment?
   What happens next week?
   What will Ricardo do in two weeks?

3. What job do you do?
   Were you ever laid off?
   How many people were laid off with you?
   Did you ever get unemployment?

4. Why does Ricardo think he's unemployed?
   Why do you think he's unemployed?
   Are there factories laying off people near you?

5. How can you get unemployment?
   Who pays for unemployment?
   Who should pay for unemployment?

Practice

I am		I was	
You are		You were	
He is	laid off.	He was	laid off.
They are		They were	
We are		We were	

Suggested Activities

1. Bring in regulations and forms for getting unemployment. List benefits on board. Practice the interview at the unemployment office.
2. Continue practice on how to find a job. Have students work with a partner to practice interviews.
3. Expand the vocabulary on feelings in a job interview.

   When I get _____, I _____.
   When I'm _____, I _____.

nervous	mumble
anxious	shake
unsure	lower my eyes
tense	talk softly
upset	yell
angry	stare
relaxed	smile
confident	sit back

6. Work in My Home Country

My name is Fidel Veran. I have been a stonemason for 35 years. I learned from my father. I learned when I was very small. The Peruvian masons are not like Americans. The Americans only know how to work with bricks. In Peru, I learned everything, from how to use a shovel to building a house.

I came to the U.S. 15 years ago. I found work with my brother. Then I found work in a small company. I have worked there for the last 8 years. Two years ago, I wanted to change jobs. I was tired of the company and wanted better wages, but I couldn't find a better job. I still work there and my wages go up a little every year.

Tools for Dialogue

1. How long has Mr. Veran been a stonemason?
   How did he learn?
   When did he come to the U.S.?
   Where did he find work first?
   Where did he find work later?

2. Does Mr. Veran like his job?
   Why did he want to change jobs?
   How is the work of a mason different in Peru and the U.S.?
   What would make his job better in the U.S.?

3. What did you do in your country?
   What was your first job in the United States?
   What is your work now? How long have you worked there?
   Is your work now different from your work in your country?
   How long have you been here?

4. In your country, is work different from the U.S.?
   How is your work different?—pay, hours, variety, relationships
   Why is work different?
   How do you learn a job in your home country?

5. What do you like better about work here?
   What do you like better about work in your home country?
   What could make your job better?

Practice

I have been	a stonemason for 35 years.
You	a painter for 7 months.
He/She has been	a teacher for 2 years.
They have been	welders for 20 years.
We	nurses for 3½ years.

I want a *better* job.
better wages.
better hours.

Suggested Activities

1. Have students write work histories, starting with work in their country and work here (include unpaid work on farm or in home).
2. Have students bring in examples of craft work from their countries to share and describe to fellow students. This allows many women who haven't worked outside the home to demonstrate their work skills.

7. Women and Work

Em: Hey, Margarita. Let's apply for promotions.
Margarita: Oh, they won't give us the packing jobs. Only men do packing.
Em: You and I need more money. Let's try.

Supervisor: What can I do for you?
Margarita: We want to apply for promotions.
Supervisor: Okay. Fill out these forms. Where do you work now?
Em: I work in section C. I sort the tomatoes.
Margarita: I fill the cans with tomato sauce.
Supervisor: How long have you worked here?
Em: We have worked here three years.
Supervisor: You have to know English to work in packing.
Margarita: We know some English.
Em: I'm studying English at night.
Supervisor: Well, I'll let you know. Other people are also applying.

Tools for Dialogue

1. What do Em and Margarita want?
   Where does Em work now?
   Where does Margarita work now?
   How long have they worked in the cannery?

2. Why do Em and Margarita want packing jobs?
   Why do they think they won't get the jobs?
   Where do women work in the cannery?
   Where do men work in the cannery?
   Who gets paid more?

3. Where do you work?
   Do you work with all women? all men?
   Have you applied for a promotion?
   Do women work in the same jobs in your workplace?
   Do men work in the same jobs in your workplace?
   What kinds of jobs did you have in your country?
   What kinds of jobs do women have in your country?

4. What jobs do women have in the United States?
   What jobs do men have in the United States?
   Why do men and women many times have different jobs?
   If a woman has the same job as a man, is she paid the same?

5. What jobs can women do?
   Can women do hard work?
   What do women want in their jobs?

Practice

I'll let you know.
I'll tell you later.
I'll call you later.

   She'll call later.
   He'll tell you later.

Suggested Activities

1. Bring in pictures of women doing all kinds of work.
2. List on board what students want in a job (pay, hours, numbers of people to work with, breaks, variety)
3. Have students role-play asking for promotions and explaining why students deserve them.

8. Safety in the Electronics Plant

Josefa: Kim, come here quickly.
 Kim: What happened?
Josefa: I got the yellow chemical in my eye. It's killing me.
 Kim: Go tell the supervisor.

Josefa: Tom! My eye really hurts.
 Tom: What did you do?
Josefa: I got the yellow chemical in my eye.
 Tom: Did you wash it out?
Josefa: Yes, but it still hurts a lot.
 Tom: It looks red.
Josefa: I can barely see. I hope I don't go blind.
 Tom: Let's go to the nurse. Maybe you should go home.
Josefa: What about my pay for today?

Tools for Dialogue

1. What happened to Josefa?
    How does her eye feel?
    Did she wash it out?
    Did water help her eye?
    Is Josefa worried?
    Does she go to the nurse?

2. Does Josefa know the name of the chemical?
    Does she know what the chemical does to her eye?
    What should Josefa do?
    Are chemicals dangerous?
    Was she protected?

3. Do you work with chemicals? What are they?
    Do you work with anything dangerous? machinery, tools, sprays, dusts?
    Are you protected?
    Do you wear anything for protection? gloves, boots, hard hats, aprons?

4. Why is Josefa not protected?
    Will she get her pay if she goes home?
    Who pays for the doctor?
    Who is responsible for Josefa's accident?

5. How can you be more protected at work?
    How can you find out about chemicals?
    Do you have training or classes about your safety and health?
    If there's an accident, what do you do? What does your employer do?
    Do you have a union?

Practice

It really hurts.
It hurts a lot.

It's hurting a lot.

	me.
	you.
It's killing	him.
	her.
	them.
	us.

Maybe you should go home.

Suggested Activities

1. Have students list on board their jobs, what's dangerous (if anything) and how they are protected. Ask how they can be more protected.
2. Bring copies of safety materials/posters/brochures to translate or interpret in class.
3. Bring in workers compensation brochures (can be obtained in many languages).
4. Explain OSHA—how workers can report unsafe conditions, retain their anonymity, etc.

9. Union

Shop steward: What's the matter?

Manager: I put Mrs. Wong on probation. She's late all the time.

Shop steward: But she's a good worker. Mrs. Wong, do you have a problem?

Mrs. Wong: My child is very sick. I have to wait for the babysitter.

Shop steward: How long have you worked here?

Mrs. Wong: I've worked here five years.

Shop steward: Is she very late?

Manager: She's been late all this month. I'm putting her on probation.

Shop steward: We'll have to file a grievance. Can you come to the union office?

Tools for Dialogue

1. What's probation?
   Why is Mrs. Wong on probation?
   Who is sick?
   Why is Mrs. Wong late?

2. How long has Mrs. Wong been late?
   How long has she worked there?
   Is she a good worker?
   Should she be on probation? Does she have a good excuse?

3. What problems do you have at work?
   How many people do you work with? Do you know them?
   How is the manager or supervisor at your work?
   Have you been on probation? Why?
   Did you have a good excuse?

4. Why are there problems at work?
   Why are there problems with managers or supervisors?

5. What can a union do? How can a union help?
   What can't a union do?
   What benefits do you get with a union? What are problems with unions?
   Do you belong to a union? Why or why not?
   Do you want to belong to a union?

Practice

	late	
	early	all week.
She's been	sick	all month.
	tired	all day.
	hungry	all morning.
	happy	

Suggested Activities

1. List on board the benefits from a union and the problems people see with unions.

2. List on board the different unions people belong to. Have one student bring in a contract to go over.

3. Contact some local unions and ask for any organizing pamphlets or informational packets (sometimes in other languages).

4. Bring in grievance form and have students roleplay asking for grievances.

VIII. MONEY OVERVIEW

Language in Money unit presented in following lesson plans, codes 1-8:

Vocabulary: quantity (1)
adjectives for food items (1, 2)
advertisements/commercials (4)
bank credit/getting a loan (5)
post office transactions (6)
budgeting—receipts (7)
taxes (8)

Language functions and structures:

make comparisons (1, 2) — sweeter than, the sweetest apple
express disbelief (3) — It couldn't be sour.
use the word "get" to mean acquire (5, 6) — get a loan, get money
express apology (5) — I'm sorry, I can't help you.

People use money every day, taking the bus to work, grabbing a cup of coffee, stopping at the food store, or paying bills. Money can be taken for granted and spent too rapidly on necessities or going out. A trip to the shopping mall often combines necessary clothes-buying with a day's entertainment.

Yet the majority of English as a Second Language students (and many Americans) cannot take money for granted. With families to support here and back home, many find themselves with little to spare. Inflation hits hardest for low-income workers, people on fixed incomes, refugees on welfare allotments, and those strapped by credit bills.

This unit discusses money as a social concern; people have basic rights to food, shelter, clothing, and work. Yet often people blame themselves for not having enough money to claim these rights.

Teachers can use this unit to look at rising food prices and discuss what people spend their money on—how do they shop, look for bargains, and budget their paycheck. Comparisons of markets and stores in the U.S. and different countries are made, including supermarkets, consumer cooperatives, and the "flea market."

Consumer protection is a major issue throughout the dialogues. If people have complaints, they need to know where to turn for help. The role of advertising in creating imaginary needs or over-selling real needs is explored. Students are asked to analyze newspaper ads and television commercials for what they do and don't tell the public. Shopping also includes selective buying or *not* buying, if there's a consumer boycott of a product. Although this unit does not contain a boycott code, teachers may discover that boycotts are a live issue for many of their students at different times.

The competency-skills in the unit include money transactions such as banking, obtaining loans, getting credit, understanding withholding taxes, and sending money and packages through the mails. Yet each transaction occurs in its real social and linguistic context. The questions ask: who can get loans, what type of references or previous credit is needed, why people use credit cards, and why people send money home when they have little money here.

The final issue concerns government services and programs that support many immigrants, refugees, and native-born Americans. Public assistance, social security, food stamps entail a distribution of funds from the government to the public. Questions look at where tax money comes from and who benefits. Why is there a stigma attached to public assistance when there aren't enough jobs to go around? Students are asked to locate public services in their neighborhoods (police, libraries, museums, health organizations) so they understand the public benefits of tax monies.

1. Food Prices

Wilson: Oh no. Not again.

Leticia: What's the matter?

Wilson: The prices at this store keep getting higher and higher.

Leticia: I know. I can't save any money.

Wilson: And I have to feed three kids.

Leticia: Mr. Brown. Why are the food prices getting higher every month?

Manager: I can't help it. The companies charge more money.

Leticia: But I don't get paid more money at work.

Wilson: Are any prices going down?

Manager: Yes, in a few weeks the summer fruits will cost less.

Leticia: What can we do? I still have to buy rice and beans and . . .

Tools for Dialogue

1. What's the matter?
   Can Leticia save any money?
   How many kids does Wilson have?
   Are any prices going down?

2. Why are the prices getting higher?
   Does Leticia get more money at work?

3. Where do you shop?
   Are prices getting higher there?
   Can you save any money?
   How much do you spend on food every week?

4. Why are prices getting higher?
   What is higher in the winter? Why?
   What is higher in the summer? Why?

5. What can you do?
   How do you find cheaper prices?
   What stores are cheaper?
   How do you find sales or bargains?
   Can you shop at a food cooperative?

Practice

Prices	higher	every month.
Apples	cheaper	at Safeway.
Oranges are	larger	at Food Mart.
Oranges	smaller	at the A & P.
Pears	sweeter	at Lucky's.

. . . is   softer
      are   harder   . . . .
           fresher

. . . is   better
      are   worse   . . . .

Suggested Activities

1. Bring in food (or pictures) to expand vocabulary through total physical response, i.e., "Hand him the apple. Give me the oranges. Put the apples in the bag," etc. Ask, "What foods do you like? What don't you like? What grows in your country? What do you miss from your country?"

2. List on board prices and quality of selected items from common stores. Regular listings in the back of the room each week make sharing of bargains possible.

3. Have students bring in sales advertisements and coupons from newspapers. Draw up a sample weekly menu from sales items and weekly listings from back of room.

4. Develop exercises on comparison shopping. Lucky's has cheap*er* apples *than* Safeway, Food Mart has *the* cheap*est*.

5. Bring in labels to compare price and quantity, such as the price per pound of a 25 lb. bag of rice vs. a minute rice package. Ask how much each item is.

6. Ask: "What do you spend money on every day? Every week? Every month? What regular bills do you pay?" Draw up sample budget. Ask, "How can you spend less?"

2. Shopping in Different Countries

My name is Rosario Gomez. I shop at the supermarket every week. Sometimes I go to Lucky's near my house. I always look in the newspaper for specials. The 7-11 store is the worst. They are always more expensive.

On Saturdays I shop at the flea market. It's cheaper than supermarkets. I can bargain there. I like it because I know people now. It is the same as the markets in Guatemala where I come from.

My name is Angelina Guzman. I live in a small town in the mountains in El Salvador. I belong to the Pipil tribe. On Sundays I go to "el mercado" with my family. We walk ten kilometers to get there.

We sell corn and yucca that we grow on our farm. Sometimes I buy rice, cheese, and sugar to take home.

I like to go to "el mercado" because I see my friends.

Tools for Dialogue

1. Where does Rosario Gomez shop?
   What store is the most expensive?
   Why does she like the flea market?
   How is it like Guatemala?

   Where does Angelina Guzman shop?
   How far does she walk to the market?
   What does she sell? What does she buy?
   Why does she like "el mercado"?

2. What's the difference between stores in the U.S. and Central America?
   How is the flea market like "el mercado"?
   Do you see friends where you shop?

3. Where do you shop? Why?
   Do you like large supermarkets?
   Where did you shop in your home country?
   Was it different? Which do you like better?

4. Why are markets different?
   Do you know people at U.S. stores?
   Where do you meet your friends here?

Practice

It's	more expensive more delicious more nutritious cheaper worse better	than . . . .

It's the	most expensive most delicious most nutritious cheapest worst best

---

Suggested Activities

1. Bring in pictures of markets and stores in different countries and the U.S. Ask: "In your country: Where did you buy produce, bread, meat, dry In the U.S.: goods, dairy products? How often did you shop? Did you barter or bargain?"

2. Bring in pictures and information on shopping cooperatives. Compare pricing and interaction in large supermarkets and small groceries.

3. Compare foods in different cultures. What do you usually eat in your country? In the U.S.? If possible, make a group exercise out of preparing a meal.

4. Have students role-play shopping at different stores. Use empty packages, foods, labels, real money. Make areas for the bakery, produce, meat depts., etc.

5. Plan a field trip to a food store. Assign tasks to each student, i.e., ask where the olives are, ask what's the freshest produce, etc. Pairing up students, one to ask and the other to listen, provides support. They can alternate parts.

3. Shopping Complaint

Husband: Hey, Rosie. The milk's sour.
   Wife: It couldn't be sour. I just bought it yesterday.
Husband: It spoiled my coffee. Here, taste it.
   Wife: Ugh, you're right. It's sour. I'll have to take it back.

   Wife: May I speak to the manager, please?
Manager: I'm the manager. How can I help you?
   Wife: I bought this milk yesterday and it's sour.
Manager: Did you check the date?
   Wife: Yes, the date on the carton is next Saturday.
Manager: Do you have a sales slip?
   Wife: No, I don't.
Manager: Well, we need the sales slip.
   Wife: But I shop here all the time.
Manager: All right. I don't know you, but I'll exchange it this one time.

Tools for Dialogue

1. When did Rosie buy the milk?
   How did the milk spoil the husband's coffee?
   What's the date on the carton?
   What does she say to the manager?

2. Does she have a sales slip?
   Does she need a sales slip?
   Can she exchange the milk?
   Does the manager want to exchange it?

3. Have you exchanged anything?
   Have you bought sour milk before? or other bad food?
   What did you do?
   Did the manager listen to you?
   Did someone help you speak English?

4. What foods have dates on them?
   Why do you check the dates?
   Why do you save sales slips?

5. When you have a complaint, what do you do?
   Does it help if you know people in the store?
   Where can you get help? Where can you write a letter of complaint?

Practice

| It couldn't be | sour.
that late.
six o'clock.
so expensive.
$10.00. | taste
sip
smell
touch
feel | it |

Suggested Activities

1. Bring in labels and cartons from dairy and meat products to check expiration dates. Have students role-play asking how fresh different foods are.

2. List on the board different kinds of shopping and complaints with merchandise, i.e., the flour has bugs, cans have bacteria, new clothes have a rip, you bought the wrong size, colors ran in a "colorfast" fabric, etc. Have students role-play going to the manager or complaints office in a department store to ask to exchange the merchandise. Discuss when you can and can't exchange.

3. Bring in information on Consumer Protection. The *Consumer's Resource Handbook* (from the White House Office of Consumer Affairs, Consumer Information Center, Dept. 532 G, Pueblo, Colorado 81009) has information on where to go for assistance (State Consumer Offices, Better Business Bureaus, Small Claims Courts, Legal Services) and how to file complaints.

4. Have students write letters of complaint.

4. Advertisements

Tools for Dialogue

1. What's in the picture?
   What does the commercial or ad say?
   Who is in the room?

2. What does the ad tell you?
   What does the ad *not* tell you?
   Where do you see ads? in the newspaper? on T.V.?
   Do you see them in your home country also?
   What's false advertising?

3. Do you watch T.V. commercials?
   Do you buy things from T.V. commercials? What?
   What do T.V. commercials want to sell you?
   What ads are there in your home country?

4. Why are there commercials on T.V.?
   Who pays for T.V. programs?

5. How can you learn about things to buy?
   How can you watch for false advertising?
   How can you make good decisions about things to buy?

Suggested Activities

1. Have students watch T.V. and bring in examples of commercials. Discuss what they tell you, what they don't tell you, what they want you to do, and if there's false advertising.

2. Bring in labels from food products advertised on T.V. or in the newspaper. Compare to other products people could substitute, i.e., coca-cola vs. milk, sugared cereal vs. non-sugar cereal, fast-food sugar/chocolate snacks vs. more nutritious snacks. Compare quality of nutrition, price and availability. The "FDA Consumer" from the Office of Public Affairs, FDA, U.S. Dept. of Health offers information on nutrition labels, i.e. what's imitation or natural foods.

3. Have people make up commercials for their favorite foods or products—crazy or serious ones.

4. Bring in Consumer Union Reports. Have students read about products they would like to buy. Ask what ads don't tell them that Consumer Union Reports does.

5. At the Bank

Bank clerk: Good morning. How are you today? Can I help you?

Martin: My name is Martin Chin. I have a savings account here and I want to take out a loan. I want to buy a car.

Bank clerk: You have to fill out an application. How much money do you need?

Martin: I need $1000.

Bank clerk: Do you have credit? Do you have any credit cards?

Martin: No, I don't.

Bank clerk: (looks at application) I see you only work seven months of the year.

Martin: Yes, my work is seasonal. I only work when it doesn't rain.

Bank clerk: Unless you have a co-signer who has better credit than you, we cannot give you a loan that large. I'm sorry.

Martin: But I don't know anyone who can sign with me. What can I do?

Bank clerk: I'm sorry. We can't help you. Maybe you should go to a Savings and Loan Association.

Martin: Will they give me credit?

Bank clerk: Their interest rate is higher, but you probably can take out a loan.

Tools for Dialogue

1. What does Martin Chin want?
   Why does he want a loan?
   Does he have an account at the bank?
   When does he work during the year?

2. Does he have credit cards?
   Can he get credit at the bank?
   Why can't he get the loan?

3. Have you taken out a loan?
   Did you have a problem?
   Did you have a co-signer?
   Do you have credit cards?
   What do you need to get credit?

4. How much do you think Martin has in his savings account?
   Where does the bank clerk advise him to go?
   Why is a Savings and Loan interest rate higher?
   Why do people need loans? (buy cars, property, home appliances . . .)
   What's good about credit?
   What's the problem with credit?

5. Where can people take out loans?
   Where can you get help to take out loans?

Practice

I		
You	can	take out a loan
He/She		get a loan
They	can't	give a loan
We		get credit

	credit
I have	good credit.
	bad credit.

Suggested Activities

1. Ask if people have credit cards, what they use them for, if they think they charge too much with credit cards, how they budget payments.
2. Ask why people need loans and credit. "What's helpful about buying on credit? What are the problems?"
3. Bring in information on credit institutions: banks, savings and loans, credit unions. Compare ease of getting a loan and interest rates.
4. Bring in a speaker (or information) from the Consumer Credit Counseling Services which offers help in budgeting and seeking credit.

6. Sending Money Home

Song: I got paid yesterday. I'm going to send money home to Vietnam.

Tham: Don't you need the money to live here?

Song: Yes, but my mother also needs money. How do I send it?

Tham: Are you sending a check?

Song: I don't have a checking account.

Tham: Go to the bank and get an international money order. Then send it from the post office.

Clerk: Can I help you?

Song: Yes please. I want to send this money order to Vietnam. How should I do it?

Clerk: You should register the letter.

Song: What's registering a letter?

Clerk: You get a receipt. If the letter gets lost, you bring the receipt to the claims department.

Song: Do I get my money back?

Clerk: Yes. It only costs a few dollars to register.

Song: Okay. I'll do it. Thank you very much.

Tools for Dialogue

1. What's Song going to do with his money?
   Does he have a checking account?
   Where does he go first?
   What's registering a letter?
   Does he keep his receipt?
   If the letter gets lost, how does he get his money back?

2. Does Song need money to live in the United States?
   Does his mother need money in Vietnam?
   Does he get enough money?

3. Do you send money home to your family?
   How do you send money? Do you send presents?
   Do you have to pay taxes on what you send?

4. Why do you send money home?
   Why do you send packages?
   Why does your family need money?
   Why can you make more money in the United States?

5. Does it help your family if you send packages from the U.S.?
   Does it help the government in your home country, if you work here in the U.S.? How?

Practice

	get paid	got paid
I	get lost	
	get back money	
	get a money order	

It gets lost

How much does it cost?
    It costs _____.

Suggested Activities

1. Have students role-play asking for information at the post office for overseas rates, sending a package and insuring it, buying stamps and airmail letters, going to the claims department if a letter or package was lost.
2. Ask students to write a letter in English to another class member and send it by mail with a properly addressed envelope.
3. Ask them to write a letter of complaint to the claims department.
4. Take a field trip to the post office and ask for different things at the window.

7. Public Assistance

Tools for Dialogue

1. What is the picture?
   Who is waiting?
   Where are they waiting?
   What do the signs say?
   What is someone saying?

2. When do people need welfare? Unemployment?
   What help can people get from the welfare/unemployment office?
   Is the wait long?
   Is the office friendly?
   Are welfare officers bilingual?
   Are the forms bilingual?

3. Do you know people who get welfare, food stamps, or unemployment?
   Do they get enough money each month?
   Is it hard to get payments?
   How does welfare make you feel?

4. Why do people need welfare, food stamps or unemployment benefits?
   Are there jobs for everybody? Why not?
   Who can't get jobs?
   If women have small children, how much is a babysitter?
   Do jobs pay enough for the babysitter?

5. How does welfare, food stamps help?
   What do you need to do to get welfare, food stamps or unemployment?
   What are the essentials—things you need every month?

Essentials Vocabulary

rent
utilities
  gas
  electricity
  water
  telephone
  transportation
  food
childcare

Suggested Activities

1. Bring in forms for general assistance, food stamps and state medical insurance for students to learn how to fill out. Role-play interviews at the welfare office. Many students may need public assistance but not know how to apply.

2. Use stories from the book *Welfare Mothers Speak Out* to initiate discussions on what is a decent living, and rights to social services.

3. Bring in speakers from the National Welfare Rights Organization or Neighborhood Legal Services.

Special Note: Teachers should be sensitive that students might not want to reveal they get welfare assistance. If people feel comfortable, they will volunteer personal information. Discussions in the third person, however, can be as useful for the students.

8. Taxes and Public Services

REGULAR HOURS	PREMIUM HOURS						PERIOD ENDING	CHECK NUMBER	
							5/15/82	068	

CURRENT PERIOD EARNINGS					DEDUCTIONS	
REGULAR	PREMIUM	VACATION		GROSS		
$950 00				$950 00	$155 05	

YEAR TO DATE								
GROSS EARNINGS	FED. WITHHOLDING	F.I.C.A.	STATE TAX 1	STATE TAX 2	CITY TAX		CHECK AMOUNT	
$950 00	$93 50	$28 75	$32 80				$794 95	

DETACH AND RETAIN THIS STATEMENT OF EARNINGS AND DEDUCTIONS FOR YOUR RECORDS
NOT NEGOTIABLE

Tools for Dialogue

1. How much does she get paid?
   How often does she get paid?
   How much money in taxes is withheld each month?
   What are the different taxes?

2. What are withholding taxes?
   What's the social security tax?
   When do you fill out income tax forms?
   When do you pay taxes from the forms?
   When do you get taxes back?

3. How much do you get paid?
   How much money is withheld each month?
   What kind of taxes are withheld?
   Did you pay taxes in your home country?

4. Why do you pay taxes here?
   When do you get social security tax money back?
   Who decides how to spend taxes?

5. What does the government do with taxes?
   What do taxes pay for?
   Think about your community; what services are paid for by taxes?

Tax Vocabulary

federal income tax
state income tax
FICA
withholding tax
  money withheld
W-4
Form 1040
Form 1040A
April 15

Suggested Activities

1. Have students bring in wage slips or make up wage slips on the board. Identify the taxes and calculate the percentage of the wages.

2. Bring in income tax forms to go over with students.

3. Ask who uses social security monies. How does social security help? Is it enough? Discuss other groups such as veterans or AFDC mothers who get direct government grants. Why do they receive tax dollars?

4. Make a list of all public services that are paid by taxes (schools, libraries, police, health services, museums). Ask what students use and what they don't use. What would happen if there were no taxes?

5. Bring in newspaper articles about tax dollars.

6. Have students walk or drive through their neighborhood and write down all services or groups paid out of tax money. Ask if students are pleased with their local services. How can they make complaints or suggestions if they aren't pleased?

7. Take a class field trip to a public service they haven't been to (the zoo, public library, museum).

A BRIEF LOOK AT THE U.S.:
A NATION OF IMMIGRANTS

ESL teachers need to know about their students: where they come from, what their concerns are, and what cultures they bring to the United States. Without this knowledge of the students, developing a curriculum and an individualized classroom environment becomes extremely difficult.

The United States is a nation of immigrants. Many history books, especially in the past, have emphasized European migrations to America, yet non-Anglo immigration has existed since America's beginnings. African slaves and hundreds of thousands of Mexican, Caribbean, Chinese, Philippine, and other Asian and Latin Americans were recruited or self-propelled to work in America. Their families and friends continue to join them either legally or illegally. Recently, refugees from Indochina, the Caribbean, and Central America have substantially augmented the ESL student population.

The majority of ESL students in adult education programs are members of working class families. A popular image of an immigrant is a young, unskilled male from the "countryside." According to 1978 immigration data, however, the majority of immigrants are in skilled trades, factory work, small businesses and crafts.[1] Moreover, more than half are women and come from urban areas. Their educational levels vary widely from little or no formal schooling to a few years of high school. Most have some degree of literacy in their own language. A small percentage—foreign students or wealthy immigrants—attend university programs for their language instruction.

Unfortunately, the demographic statistics important to us as ESL teachers are extremely difficult to obtain. Immigration data by itself is misleading, and figures on ESL students are merged into adult education or K–12 figures. Nevertheless, the immigration statistics of the last decade provide an interesting overview of the changing American population.

From 1971–1978, not counting refugees or undocumented persons, 41% of U.S. immigrants came from Latin America—mostly Mexico and the West Indies—34.5% from Asia, and 19% from Europe, for a total of 3.5 million people. The shift in population from the previous decade is striking. Between 1961 and 1970, twice as many people came from Europe, only 13% from Asia, a slightly lower percentage from Latin America, with a comparable total of 3.3 million people. The increase of Asian immigrants in the seventies has risen steeply with the 600,000 Indochinese refugees who have arrived since 1975. Cuban refugees arriving during the past decade (over 360,000) have raised the percentage of Latin Americans.

Not counted in these immigration figures are the important group of undocumented persons, largely from Mexico. (Current estimates range from five to ten million people residing without papers in the United States.) Testimony before the Senate Judiciary Subcommittee in Fall 1981 suggested that 250,000 to 500,000 undocumented persons enter the United States each year.[2] Though many attend ESL classes, the majority do not. The fear of exposure and deportation prohibits illegals from registering for class, especially if schools strictly enforce requirements for students having legal status. Many of the undocumented would apply for permanent residence were it not for the several year backlog of paperwork at the Immigration and Naturalization Service.

Other untold numbers of refugees, fleeing from Central America and Haiti, are not granted the political refugee status required for legal residence. While nearly 100% of the Indochinese are given political refugee papers, less than 3% of the Central Americans who apply for asylum are considered legitimate political refugees. With no other legal alternative, Central Americans attempt to enter the United States without visas. For Salvadorans alone, the figures range from 200,000 to 500,000 now living in the United States.

As of 1982, immigration policy on the status of undocumented persons is under review. Some proposals suggest granting *de facto* residency for those who can prove they have lived here for five years. Others offer "guest worker" programs that woud legalize a percentage of the steady illegal immigration. If any of the proposals are enacted, the need for ESL classes would grow rapidly. As teachers, we would face the difficult task of encouraging the new students, who had lived in relative isolation, to interact with Anglo society. Our curriculum would then have to reflect these students' new difficulties and hopes.

In addition to immigration data, a National Center for Education Statistics (NCES) study in 1977 gives more information on who qualifies for ESL classes.[3] The study found that one in eight persons living in the United States (28 million people) have non-English language backgrounds—this figure includes people who speak another language in their home or whose mother tongue is not English. Contrary to popular belief, the majority are not foreign born; two out of three of these persons were born in the U.S. (including Puerto Rico and U.S. territories). Of these 28 million, 10.6 come from Spanish language backgrounds. (*1980 census data adds another 4 million Latinos.*) Of the other large groups, two to three million come from Italian, German, French, and Asian backgrounds. (Again, the recent Indochinese refugees increase the number of Asians.) Approximately three million speak no English at all.

Despite the large numbers of U.S. born non-English speakers, this book often refers to the immigration experience of ESL students. First- and second-generation children of immigrant backgrounds often identify with their parents' home countries; the cultural and social conflicts of this population therefore parallel those of immigrants.

Non-English speakers (whether immigrants or many generations of U.S. born children) can best be understood in their larger historical context. Certain regional groups have had English imposed upon them as the dominant language. Until U.S. annexation in 1848, the Southwest originally belonged to Mexico; Mexicans born in the area before the Mexican-American War were guaranteed full rights of U.S. citizenship under the Treaty of Guadalupe Hidalgo. Ironically, their descendants (who may or may not speak English) are regarded as aliens. This treaty guaranteed that the Southwest would remain a bilingual/bicultural area: "Mexicans would have special privileges derived from their customs, language, law, and religions." These provisions, however, have rarely been honored.[4] Until recently, statutes denied Chicano children the right to speak Spanish in the classroom or to come to school with a non-Anglo appearance.[5] Others have had English imposed on them— Puerto Ricans, Native Americans, French-speaking (Cajun) peoples in Louisiana, and Micronesians.

The statistics speak to the magnitude of people living in language-segregated environments in homes and communities. They remind us of the importance of providing ESL classes for U.S. born non-English speakers as well as immigrants. But do ESL classes reach the U.S. born? A 1979 Ford Foundation report on illiteracy suggests that the adult education system does not reach the majority of Americans with less than a high school education. Minority group members, including ESL or potential ESL students, "will never enroll in programs of any sort for diverse reasons: cultural or linguistic barriers, fear of failing, distrust of the institutions of mainstream culture."[6]

Our responsibility then as ESL teachers and administrators is to provide programs for current and potential ESL students that address the cultural, linguistic, physical, emotional, and social barriers to learning. These programs may include problem-posing curricula, bilingual classes, cultural activities, and community action. Only then will students increase their ability to participate democratically in U.S. society.

FOOTNOTES TO A BRIEF LOOK AT THE U.S.:
A NATION OF IMMIGRANTS

1. "Immigration and Naturalization," *Statistical Abstract of the United States*, 101st Edition, Census Bureau, U.S. Dept. of Commerce, 1980, pp. 89–100.

2. "Critics Say 'Guest Worker' Plan Won't Halt Illegal Immigrants," *Albuquerque Journal*, October 23, 1981, p. A-20.

3. "Non-English Language Background Persons: Three U.S. Surveys," *TESOL Quarterly*, Vol. 12, No. 3, September 1978, pp. 247–261.

4. "Treaty of Guadalupe Hidalgo, 1848," articles 8 and 19. *Mexican-American Source Book*, ed. Feliciano Rivera, Menlo Park, CA: Educational Consulting Associates, 1970.

5. Dunaway, David, "Teaching Reading and Composition More Efficiently: A Language Approach for Teachers," STRIDE Project, Far West Laboratory for Educational Research and Development, San Francisco, 1976.

6. Hunter, Carman St. John, and Harman, David, *Adult Illiteracy in the United States, A Report to the Ford Foundation*, New York: McGraw-Hill, 1979.

RESOURCES
Materials for Classroom Use

1. Survival-oriented resources:

Forms: Job applications, driver's license tests, welfare/social service forms, bank loan/credit applications, school registrations, etc.

Newspapers/journals/foreign language newspapers/T.V. guides/telephone books

Bills/checks/wage slips/receipts

Labels from food packages/medicines/cigarettes, etc.

Consumer pamphlets/posters

Sponsor's handbook and other brochures from community agencies

Citizenship materials and other governmental information

Cookbooks from different countries/menus from restaurants

Maps/atlases/tourist guides of city

Photographs: magazines from home, *National Geographics* from second-hand shops, family photographs, art prints, pictures from public library archives

Union contracts of students/workers' compensation brochures

Manual for the Bilingual Secretary in the Community, Esther Perez, Aztlan Today Co., El Dorado Distributors, San Francisco (for Spanish-speaking).

2. Children's books (if not condescending; there are many to choose from):

Soy Chicano, I Am Mexican-American, Bob and Lynne Fitch, Creative Educational Society, Inc., Minnesota (story of Chicana growing up in agricultural valley with simple English, discussions on culture).

Todo el Mundo, Aqui y Alla en California, Ernesto Galarza, part of the Coleccion de Mini-Libros series, El Dorado Distributors, San Francisco (collection of booklets in Spanish containing short scenarios about California and Mexico; vignettes can be translated into English for side-by-side bilingual lessons).

Yo Puertoriqueño, Awilda Orta and A. C. Sheridan, Scott Foresman, Illinois, 1972 (bilingual description of Puerto Rico with fill-in blanks).

3. Stories from oral history books

Hillbilly Women, Kathy Kahn. New York: Avon, 1973 (talks with mountain women).

Life Story of the Mexican Immigrant, autobiographical documents collected by Manuel Gamio. New York: Dover Publications, 1971 (stories of economic readjustment, assimilation, changing identity . . .).

Las Mujeres, Conversations from a Hispanic Community, N. Elsasser, K. MacKenzie, Y. Tixier Y Vigil. New York: Feminist Press and McGraw-Hill, 1980.

Longtime Californ', A Documentary Study of an American Chinatown, Victor G. and Brett de Bary Nee. New York: Pantheon Books, 1972.

Terkel, Studs, *Working*. New York: Avon, 1975.

———, *Division Street: America*. New York: Pantheon Books, 1966.

4. Poetry and literature (from other countries and from cultures in the U.S.)

5. ESL Materials to draw from:

Andrews, John, *Say What You Mean in English, Book 1*. Britain: Thomas Nelson and Sons Ltd., 1975 (notional-functional text).

Asher, James J., *Learning Another Language Through Actions, Complete Teacher's Guidebook*. San Francisco: Alemany Press (total physical response).

Bodman, J. and Lanzano, M., *No Hot Water Tonight*. New York: Collier MacMillan, 1979.

Carver, Tina K. and Fotinos, Sandra D., *A Conversation Book: English in Everyday Life, Books I and II*. Englewood Cliffs, N.J.: Prentice-Hall, 1977.

Dubin, Fraida and Margol, Myrna, *It's Time to Talk*, "Communication Activities for Learning English as a New Language." Englewood Cliffs, N.J.: Prentice-Hall, 1977.

Galyean, Beverly-Colleene, *Language From Within: Handbook of teaching strategies for personal growth and self-reflection in the language class*. Long Beach, CA: Ken Zel Consultant Services, March 1976.

Graham, Carolyn, *Jazz Chants*. New York: Oxford University Press, 1978.

Harding, Deborah and Delisle, Gilles, *A Microwave Course in ESL* (for Mexican-American Migrants). La Jolla, CA: Lingoco Corporation, 1968.

Hines, M., *Skits in English*. New York: Regents Publishing Co., 1980 (skits for homes and community, doesn't include work).

Kettering, Judith, *Interaction Activities in ESL* University of Pittsburgh Press (role-play techniques).

Moskowitz, Gertrude, *Caring and Sharing in the Foreign Language Class*. Rowley, Massachusetts: Newbury House Publishers (sourcebook on Humanistic Techniques).

Olsen, Judy E. Winn-Bell, *Communication Starters and Other Activities for the ESL Classroom*. San Francisco: Alemany Press, 1977 (peer activities).

Romijn, Elizabeth and Seely, Contee, *Live Action English*. San Francisco: Alemany Press, 1980.

Educational Philosophy and Applications of Problem-Posing

Alschuler, Alfred, *School Discipline, A Socially Literate Solution*. New York: McGraw-Hill, 1980 (high school application, discipline resolution through dialogue between teachers, students, administrators).

Apperception–Interaction Method (AIM), Stories and Pictures. New York: World Education Center (ABE/GED materials at 4th grade reading level, language experience for adults).

Barndt, Deborah, *Making and Using Photo-Stories*. Toronto, Canada: Participatory Research Group, International Council of Adult Education (step-by-step account of making photo-stories with students).

———, *Education and Social Change, A Photographic Study of Peru*. Kendall/Hunt Publishing Co., 1980 (text and photo description of a problem-posing literacy program in Peru).

Brown, Cynthia, *Literacy in 30 Hours, Paulo Freire's Process in NorthEast Brazil.* London: Writers and Readers Publishing Cooperative, 1975. Reprinted in part in *Social Policy*, July/August, 1975 (Brazilian materials, interviews on applications to elementary school children).

Condon, Camy, "Multicultural Participatory Puppetry." San Diego, CA (cultural awareness training, English as a Second Language technique, community issues).

Conti, Gary, "Rebels With a Cause: Myles Horton and Paulo Freire," *Community College Review*, 5, Summer, 1977.

Crone, Catherine and Hunter, Carman St. John, *From the Field: Tested Participatory Activities for Trainers.* New York: World Education Center, 1980 (learners' needs assessment, materials development, discussion techniques).

Drummond, Therese, *Using the Method of Paulo Freire in Nutrition Education: An Experimental Plan for Community Action in Northeast Brazil.* New York: Cornell International Nutrition Monograph Series, No. 3, Cornell University, 1975.

Dunaway, David, "Teaching Reading and Composition More Efficiently: A Language Approach for Teachers." San Francisco: Far West Laboratory for Educational Research and Development, STRIDE Project, 1976 (training manual on language attitudes and differences).

Duncombe, Brenda, et al., *Themes for Learning and Teaching.* Toronto, Canada: ESL Core Group, 1979 (ESL curriculum divided into problem themes).

Elsasser, N. and V. John-Steiner, "An Interactionist Approach to Advancing Literacy," *Harvard Educational Review*, Vol. 47, No. 3, 1977.

Fiore, Kyle and Elsasser, N., "Strangers No More: A Liberatory Literacy Curriculum," *College English*, Jan., Feb., 1982.

Frankenstein, Marilyn, "A Different Third R: Radical Math." Boston: University Mass., March, 1981 (teaching techniques for social literacy through arithmetic).

Freire, Paulo, *Cultural Action for Freedom.* Center for the Study of Development and Social Change, Cambridge, Mass., 1970. Reprinted from *Harvard Educational Review*, XL, May and August, 1970.

———, *Pedagogy of the Oppressed.* New York: Seabury Press, 1970 (Freire's major theoretical text, the first to be translated into English).

———, *Conscientization and Liberation.* Geneva: Institute of Cultural Action, 1972.

———, *Education for Critical Consciousness.* New York: Seabury Press, 1973 (contains the essay, "Education as the Practice of Freedom," explaining the literacy method in concrete terms).

———, *Pedagogy in Process: The Letters to Guinea Bissau.* New York: Seabury Press, 1978 (description of collaborative work with government in organizing literacy program, ideological and methodological considerations).

———, "By Learning They Can Teach." *Convergence*, Vol. 6, No. 1, 1973 (dialogue as liberating education).

———, "To the Coordinator of a Cultural Circle." *Convergence*, Vol. 4, No. 1, 1974 (role of teachers as facilitators).

Hirschman, Sarah, *Gente y Cuentos* (People and Stories), Reston, Virginia: Project of Latino Institute, 1981 (unpublished text of dialogue method using Spanish short stories, for ESL or Spanish literacy).

"Holdings on Adult Literacy and Related Topics," bibliography compiled by Newcomer Services Branch, Ministry of Culture and Recreation, Toronto, Canada, 1980.

Horton, Myles, *Unearthing Seeds of Fire: The Idea of Highlander*, by Frank Adams with M. Horton. Winston-Salem, N.C., 1975 (autobiographical account of founder of Highlander Education and Research Center, New Market, Tennessee, that has operated adult education and community self-development programs since the 1930s).

Hunter, Carman St. John and Harman, David, *Adult Illiteracy in the United States*, A Report to the Ford Foundation. New York: McGraw Hill, 1979 (analysis of illiteracy problems).

James, Michael, "A New Way to Teach, A New Way to Learn: The First Nine Months." San Francisco: Project for Literacy Education, 1980 (applications to high school).

Kalmar, Tomas, "Evri Bari Guants Tulem, Working Paper #5" (Every Body Wants to Learn), Carbondale, Illinois Migrant Council, 1980 (bilingual literacy method and campaign).

Kohl, Herbert, *Reading, How To.* New York: Dutton and Company, 1973.

Kozol, Jonathan, *Prisoners of Silence: Breaking the Bonds of Adult Illiteracy in the United States.* New York: Seabury Press, 1980.

London, Jack, "Reflections Upon the Relevance of Paulo Freire for American Adult Education," in *Paulo Freire: A Revolutionary Dilemma for the Adult Educator*, ed. Stanley Grabowski. ERIC Clearinghouse on Adult Education Occasional Papers #32, November, 1972.

Luttrel, Wendy, *Women in the Community.* Philadelphia: Women's Program, Lutheran Settlement House (GED/ABE curriculum for women's re-entry program).

Marcus, Lotte, *AKTOS* and English on Wheels materials. Carmel, CA (ESL curriculum for migrant farmworkers based on cultural communication and miscommunication, creative use of role plays and videos).

McFadden, John, "Consciousness and Social Change, The Pedagogy of Paulo Freire." Ph.D. dissertation, School of Education, California State University, Sacramento, 1975.

Minkler, Meredith and Kathleen Cox, "Creating Critical Consciousness in Health." *International Journal of Health Services*, Vol. 10, No. 2, 1980 (application to health care with elderly poor in San Francisco, and rural health workers in Honduras).

Moriarty, Pia, "ESL/Literacy Teaching Strategy and Curriculum Outline." San Francisco, 1979 (problem-posing applied to literacy Indochinese students).

Moriarty, Pia and Wallerstein, Nina, "By Teaching We Can Learn: Freire Process for Teachers." *California Journal of Teacher Education*, Winter, 1980 (teacher training).

Moriarty, Pia and Wallerstein, Nina, "Student/Teacher/Learner: A Freire Approach to ABE/ESL." *Adult Literacy and Basic Education*, Fall, 1979.

Multicultural Education: A Cross-cultural Training Approach, ed. Margaret D. Pusch. Chicago: Intercultural Press, Inc. (invaluable teacher training methods for developing multicultural programs).

Nyere, Julius, "Declaration of Dar Es Salaam and Design for Action." *Convergence*, Vol. 9, No. 4, 1976 (statement by President of Tanzania on five-year plan for a national adult education program).

Partners in Learning, *South Dade Labor Camp, Primer 1*, developed by B. Machado, Miami: Florida International University, 1981 (photographs and very beginning ESL for migrant farmworkers).

Partners in Learning with Liberacion Learning Center, *Clown Manual*, developed by J. Mossman, 1980 (clowning in liberatory education).

Postman, Neil and Weingartner, Charles, *Teaching as a Subversive Activity*. New York: Dell Publishing Co., 1969.

Rosten, Leo, *The Education of H*Y*M*A*N K*A*P*L*A*N*, by Leonard Ross (pseud.). New York: Harcourt Brace, 1937; later reissued, New York: Harper and Row, 1976.

Saville-Troike, Muriel, *Foundations for Teaching English as a Second Language: Theory and Method for Multicultural Education*. New Jersey: Prentice-Hall, 1976 (philosophical, psychological and educational rationale for multicultural education).

Shor, Ira, *Critical Teaching and Everyday Life*. Boston: South End Press, 1980 (problem-posing teaching with working class students in open admissions community college setting in New York).

Shuy, Roger, "Relevance of Socio-Linguistics for Language Teaching." *TESOL Quarterly*, Vol. 3, No. 1, March, 1969 (social implications of language use).

"Silabario." New York: Solidaridad Humana, 1980 (literacy curriculum for Spanish-speakers, based on reality of lower East Side, New York).

Smith, Frank, *Understanding Reading*. New York: Holt, Rinehart and Winston, 1978.

Taba, Hilda, "The Teaching of Thinking." *Elementary English*, XLII, May, 1965 (summary of Taba's research with description of questioning strategies).

———, et al., *A Teacher's Handbook to Elementary Social Studies: An Inductive Approach*. Menlo Park, CA: Addison-Wesley, 1971 (teacher's guide to elementary school studies curriculum that teaches children inductive questioning format similar to Freire's problem-posing with adults).

Themes and Tools for ESL: How To Choose Them and How To Use Them, compiled by Deborah Barndt, distributed by Ministry of Culture and Recreation, Citizenship Branch, Toronto, Canada (handbook on developing themes into curriculum).

Unda, Jean, et al., "Juan Manuel Looks for a Job." Toronto, Canada: Adult Services Unit, St. Christopher House, 1979 (student photo story and teacher materials in newspaper format developed by an English as a Second Language class).

Unda, Jean, "An Approach to Language and Orientation." *TESL talk*, Vol. 11, No. 4, Fall, 1980, Ontario Ministry of Culture and Recreation (syllabus design and classroom practice for problem-posing ESL and orientation classes).

Werner, David, *Where There Is No Doctor*. Palo Alto, CA: The Hesperian Foundation, 1977 (community-based primary care manual, available in many languages).

Wilkins, D. A., *Notional Syllabuses*. London: Oxford University Press, 1976.

Journals:

Convergence, quarterly journal that describes Freire projects around world, published by International Council for Adult Education, Toronto, Canada.

Educacion Liberadora, monthly newsletter linking many Freire projects in the U.S., especially those working with Spanish-speaking people; funded through FIPSE. Latino Institute, Reston, Virginia.

Non-Formal Education Exchange, newsletter that focuses on non-formal adult education and community self-development programs around the world. College of Education, Michigan State University.

Background to Different Cultures

1. General Culture:

Beals, Alan and Spindler, George and Louise, *Culture in Process*, Second Edition. New York: Holt, Rinehart and Winston, 1973 (questions in cultural anthropology).

Berger, John, *A Seventh Man*, with photographs by Jean Mohr. New York: Viking Press, 1975 (photo/prose essay of the European migrant workers' experience).

Condon, John and Yousef, Fathi, *An Introduction to Intercultural Communication*. Indianapolis: Bobbs Merrill, 1975 (standard text on the process of intercultural communication, cultural behaviors, and value orientations).

The Ethnic Almanac by Stephanie Bernardo. New York: Doubleday, 1981 (compilation of history and material culture of immigrant groups to the U.S.).

Every Man His Way, ed. Alan Dundes. New Jersey: Prentice-Hall, 1968 (readings in cultural anthropology).

Geertz, Clifford, *The Interpretation of Cultures*. New York: Basic Books, 1973 (selected essays on the theory of culture).

Hall, Edward T., *The Hidden Dimension*. New York: Doubleday, 1969.

——— , *Beyond Culture*. New York: Doubleday, 1976.

——— , *The Silent Language*. New York: Doubleday, 1959.

2. Latin American and Caribbean peoples:

Acuña, Rodolfo, *Occupied America*. New York: Harper and Row, 1980 (history of Chicanos, economic and political domination within the U.S., current political movements).

Anaya, Rudolfo, *Bless Me Ultima*. Berkeley: Tonatiuh International Publishers of Chicano Literature, 1972 (southwest novel).

Aztlan, An Anthology of Mexican-American Literature, ed. Luiz Valdez and Stan Steiner. New York: Vintage Books, 1972.

Bibliografia de Aztlan, ed. Ernie Barrios. San Diego, CA: Centro de Estudios, Chicanos Publications (literature and history bibliography).

Chicano, Caricature to Self-Portrait, ed. Edward Simmen. New York: Mentor Books, 1971 (collection of stories).

Cuentos, Tales from the Hispanic Southwest, collected by Jose Griego y Maestas and Rudolfo A. Anaya, Santa Fe: Museum of New Mexico Press (bilingual stories).

Galarza, Ernesto, et al., *Mexican-Americans in the Southwest*. Santa Barbara, CA: McNally, 1970.

Ghosts in the Barrio: Issues in Bilingual-Bicultural Education, ed. Ralph Poblano. San Rafael, CA: Leswing Press, 1973 (anthology of Chicano educators).

Introduction to Chicano Studies, ed. Livie Isauro Duran and H. Russell Bernard. New York: MacMillan Pub. Co., 1973 (articles on internal culture and relations to external world).

La Mujer, En Pie de Lucha y La Hora Es Ya, Dorinda Moreno Espina. Mexico: Del Norte Publications, 1973; El Dorado Distributors, San Francisco (bibliography of women's issues).

McWilliams, Carey, *Factories in the Fields*. Santa Barbara, CA: Peregrine Press, 1971 (analysis of agribusiness and farmworkers).

———, *North from Mexico*. Philadelphia: J. B. Lippencott Co., 1949 (history of immigrations northward, social and economic factors).

NACLA Report on the Americas (North American Congress on Latin America, bi-monthly report, published in New York)
- —"Caribbean Migration: Contract Labor in U.S. Agriculture," Vol. XI, No. 8, November/December, 1977.
- —"Going Foreign: Causes of Jamaican Migration," Vol. XV, No. 1, January/February, 1981.
- —"Undocumented: Immigrant Workers in New York City," Vol. XII, No. 6, November/December 1979.

Raza Cultural Events Series, collection of bilingual culture units celebrating raza holidays and historical figures. Berkeley, CA: B.A.B.E.L. Media Center (useful as resource or as classroom materials, send for catalogue).

Songs and Dreams, Mexican-American Literature, ed. Joseph Flores. Connecticut: Pendulum Press.

Taylor, Ronald B., *Sweatshops in the Sun: Child Labor on the Farm*. Boston: Beacon Press, 1973 (moving account of harsh conditions for over 800,000 children in the U.S.).

"Treaty of Guadalupe Hidalgo, 1848," in *Mexican-American Source Book*, ed. Feliciano Rivera. Menlo Park, CA: Educational Consulting Associates, 1970.

Understanding Spanish-Speaking Cultures, Joseph R. Scott, Alameda County School Department, CA, 1972 (how to teach culture, meaning of language in culture).

Indochinese Peoples:

The Boat People, an "Age" Investigation with Bruce Grant. England: Penguin Books, 1979 (special international reports from the foreign correspondent of the Australian newspaper, the *Age*).

FitzGerald, Frances, *Fire in the Lake, The Vietnamese and the Americans in Vietnam*. Boston: Little, Brown, 1972.

Indochinese "ESL Workbook Series: Job Search, Hello Community, New Directions, Your New Community, Teacher's Guide," Louise Locketz, Adult Community Education Center, St. Paul, Minnesota (survival workbook series designed originally for Hmong students).

Indochinese Materials Center "Bibliography," U.S. Department of Education, Kansas City, Missouri (listing of over 400 teacher's guides and curriculum materials for teaching Indochinese students).

Indochinese Patients: Cultural Aspects of Medical and Psychiatric Care for Indochinese Refugees, by Dr. Tran Minh Tung, SEAPA, Falls Church, Virginia, 1980.

Indochinese Refugee Education Guides
Adult Education Series, including "Teaching English to Adult Refugees" and "Selected Annotated Bibliography of Materials for Teaching ESL to Indochinese Refugee Adults," Summer 1979.
General Information Series, including articles on Indochinese languages and cultures.
Available from National Indochinese Clearinghouse, Center for Applied Linguistics, Washington, D.C.

Manual for Indochinese Refugee Education, 1976–77. Washington, D.C.: National Indochinese Clearinghouse Center for Applied Linguistics.

Transcultural Look at Health Care: Indochinese with Pulmonary Disease, from symposium for nurses and other health care providers, Lung Association of Mid-Maryland, Rockville, MD, 1980 (articles on cross-cultural communication, Indochinese cultures, and particular health needs and beliefs of Indochinese).

Asian-American Peoples — Chinese-, Japanese-, Filipino-, Korean-Americans:
Asian-American Curriculum Guide: Elementary and Secondary School. Minnesota: St. Paul Public Schools, June 1980 (integrating Asian-American curriculum into the classroom).

Asian-Americans, Psychological Perspectives, ed. Stanley Sue, Nathaniel Wagner. Palo Alto, CA: Science and Behavior Books, Inc., 1973 (articles on assimilation, identity, mental health, contemporary issues).

Counterpoint: Perspectives on Asian-Americans, ed. Emma Gee. Los Angeles: UCLA Asian-American Studies Program, 1976.

Houston, Jeanne Wakatsuki and James D., Farewell to Manzanar. Boston: Houghton-Mifflin, 1973 (true story of the Japanese-American experience during and after World War II internment).

Kingston, Maxine Hong, Woman Warrior, Memoirs of a Girlhood Among Ghosts. New York: Ballantine Books, 1981.

___ China Men. New York: Vintage Books, 1976.

___ H.L., Japanese-Americans: The Evolution of a Subculture. Englewood Cliffs,
___ 1969. ___ Village Series, Pantheon Books, 1973.
___ Study of an American Chinatown, Victor G. and Brett
___ ed States." Pacific Historical Review, Vol. 43, No. 4,
___ ica. New York: Harper, Colophon
___ migration).
___ ." Amerasia Journal, Vol. 4,

REFERENCES

Asher, James J. Learning Another Language Through Actions: Complet[e]... San Francisco: Alemany Press,

Crone, Catherine and Hunter, Carman St. John. From the... Activities for Trainers. New York: World Education Cen[ter]...

"El Lavaplatos" (The Dishwasher) a song performed by F... record Texas-Mexican Border Music, Vol. 2, Early Corr...

Freire, Paulo. Pedagogy of the Oppressed. New York: Seab[ury]...

___ . To the Coordinator of a Culture Circle. Conv[ergence]...

___ . By Learning They Can Teach. Convergence...

___ . Education as the Practice of Freedom.... York: Seabury Press, 1973.

___ . Pedagogy in Process: The Letters to Guin...

Gamio, Manuel. Life Story of the Mexican I[mmigrant]...

Graham, Carolyn. Jazz Chants for Chr... New York: Oxford Universi[ty]...

Hall, Edward T. Beyond Culture...

Kalmar, Tomas. "Evri Bari G[v]..." Carbondale, Illinois...

Romijn, Elizabeth and... Press, 1980.

Smalley, William A... Practical A[nthropology]...

Taba, Hilda...

Winn-Bell... S...

Galarza, Ernesto, et al., *Mexican-Americans in the Southwest*. Santa Barbara, CA: McNally, 1970.

Ghosts in the Barrio: Issues in Bilingual-Bicultural Education, ed. Ralph Poblano. San Rafael, CA: Leswing Press, 1973 (anthology of Chicano educators).

Introduction to Chicano Studies, ed. Livie Isauro Duran and H. Russell Bernard. New York: MacMillan Pub. Co., 1973 (articles on internal culture and relations to external world).

La Mujer, En Pie de Lucha y La Hora Es Ya, Dorinda Moreno Espina. Mexico: Del Norte Publications, 1973; El Dorado Distributors, San Francisco (bibliography of women's issues).

McWilliams, Carey, *Factories in the Fields*. Santa Barbara, CA: Peregrine Press, 1971 (analysis of agribusiness and farmworkers).

————, *North from Mexico*. Philadelphia: J. B. Lippencott Co., 1949 (history of immigrations northward, social and economic factors).

NACLA Report on the Americas (North American Congress on Latin America, bi-monthly report, published in New York)
—"Caribbean Migration: Contract Labor in U.S. Agriculture," Vol. XI, No. 8, November/December, 1977.
—"Going Foreign: Causes of Jamaican Migration," Vol. XV, No. 1, January/February, 1981.
—"Undocumented: Immigrant Workers in New York City," Vol. XII, No. 6, November/December 1979.

Raza Cultural Events Series, collection of bilingual culture units celebrating raza holidays and historical figures. Berkeley, CA: B.A.B.E.L. Media Center (useful as resource or as classroom materials, send for catalogue).

Songs and Dreams, Mexican-American Literature, ed. Joseph Flores. Connecticut: Pendulum Press.

Taylor, Ronald B., *Sweatshops in the Sun: Child Labor on the Farm*. Boston: Beacon Press, 1973 (moving account of harsh conditions for over 800,000 children in the U.S.).

"Treaty of Guadalupe Hidalgo, 1848," in *Mexican-American Source Book*, ed. Feliciano Rivera. Menlo Park, CA: Educational Consulting Associates, 1970.

Understanding Spanish-Speaking Cultures, Joseph R. Scott, Alameda County School Department, CA, 1972 (how to teach culture, meaning of language in culture).

Indochinese Peoples:

The Boat People, an "Age" Investigation with Bruce Grant. England: Penguin Books, 1979 (special international reports from the foreign correspondent of the Australian newspaper, the *Age*).

FitzGerald, Frances, *Fire in the Lake, The Vietnamese and the Americans in Vietnam*. Boston: Little, Brown, 1972.

Indochinese "ESL Workbook Series: Job Search, Hello Community, New Directions, Your New Community, Teacher's Guide," Louise Locketz, Adult Community Education Center, St. Paul, Minnesota (survival workbook series designed originally for Hmong students).

Indochinese Materials Center "Bibliography," U.S. Department of Education, Kansas City, Missouri (listing of over 400 teacher's guides and curriculum materials for teaching Indochinese students).

Indochinese Patients: Cultural Aspects of Medical and Psychiatric Care for Indochinese Refugees, by Dr. Tran Minh Tung, SEAPA, Falls Church, Virginia, 1980.

Indochinese Refugee Education Guides
    Adult Education Series, including "Teaching English to Adult Refugees" and "Selected Annotated Bibliography of Materials for Teaching ESL to Indochinese Refugee Adults," Summer 1979.
    General Information Series, including articles on Indochinese languages and cultures.
Available from National Indochinese Clearinghouse, Center for Applied Linguistics, Washington, D.C.

Manual for Indochinese Refugee Education, 1976–77. Washington, D.C.: National Indochinese Clearinghouse Center for Applied Linguistics.

Transcultural Look at Health Care: Indochinese with Pulmonary Disease, from symposium for nurses and other health care providers, Lung Association of Mid-Maryland, Rockville, MD, 1980 (articles on cross-cultural communication, Indochinese cultures, and particular health needs and beliefs of Indochinese).

Asian-American Peoples — Chinese-, Japanese-, Filipino-, Korean-Americans:

Asian-American Curriculum Guide: Elementary and Secondary School. Minnesota: St. Paul Public Schools, June 1980 (integrating Asian-American curriculum into the classroom).

Asian-Americans, Psychological Perspectives, ed. Stanley Sue, Nathaniel Wagner. Palo Alto, CA: Science and Behavior Books, Inc., 1973 (articles on assimilation, identity, mental health, contemporary issues).

Counterpoint: Perspectives on Asian-Americans, ed. Emma Gee. Los Angeles: UCLA Asian-American Studies Program, 1976.

Houston, Jeanne Wakatsuki and James D., *Farewell to Manzanar*. Boston: Houghton-Mifflin, 1973 (true story of the Japanese-American experience during and after World War II internment).

Kingston, Maxine Hong, *Woman Warrior, Memoirs of a Girlhood Among Ghosts*. New York: Vintage Books, 1976.

——— , *China Men*. New York: Ballantine Books, 1981.

Kitano, H. H. L., *Japanese-Americans: The Evolution of a Subculture*. Englewood Cliffs, N.J.: Prentice-Hall, 1969.

Longtime Californ', *A Documentary Study of an American Chinatown*, Victor G. and Brett de Barry Nee. New York: Pantheon Village Series, Pantheon Books, 1973.

Melendy, H. B., "Filipinos in the United States." *Pacific Historical Review*, Vol. 43, No. 4, 1974, pp. 520–547.

Steiner, Stan, *Fusang, The Chinese Who Built America*. New York: Harper, Colophon Books, 1979 (historical volume on Asian-American immigration).

Yu, E. Y., "Koreans in America: An Emerging Ethnic Minority." *Amerasia Journal*, Vol. 4, No. 1, 1977, pp. 117–131.

REFERENCES

Asher, James J. *Learning Another Language Through Actions: Complete Teacher's Guidebook.* San Francisco: Alemany Press,

Crone, Catherine and Hunter, Carman St. John. *From the Field: Tested Participatory Activities for Trainers.* New York: World Education Center, 1980.

"El Lavaplatos" (The Dishwasher) a song performed by Hermanos Banuelos, on the record *Texas-Mexican Border Music, Vol. 2, Early Corridos,* Folk Lyric Label 9004.

Freire, Paulo. *Pedagogy of the Oppressed.* New York: Seabury Press, 1970.

————. To the Coordinator of a Culture Circle. *Convergence* 4, 1 (1971): 61–62.

————. By Learning They Can Teach. *Convergence* 61, 1(1973): 78–84.

————. Education as the Practice of Freedom. *Education for Critical Consciousness.* New York: Seabury Press, 1973.

————. *Pedagogy in Process: The Letters to Guinea Bissau.* New York: Seabury Press, 1978.

Gamio, Manuel. *Life Story of the Mexican Immigrant.* New York: Dover Publications, 1971.

Graham, Carolyn. *Jazz Chants for Children: Rhythms of American English Through Chants.* New York: Oxford University Press, 1978.

Hall, Edward T. *Beyond Culture.* New York: Doubleday, 1976.

Kalmar, Tomas. "*Evri Bari Guants Tulen, Working Paper #5*" (Everybody Wants To Learn). Carbondale, Illinois Migrant Council, 1980.

Romijn, Elizabeth and Seely, Contee. *Live Action English.* San Francisco: Alemany Press, 1980.

Smalley, William A. Culture Shock, Language Shock, and the Shock of Self-Discovery. *Practical Anthropology* 10, 2 (March–April 1963): 49–56.

Taba, Hilda. The Teaching of Thinking. *Elementary English* XLII (May 1965).

Winn-Bell Olson, Judy E. *Communication Starters and Other Activities for the ESL Classroom.* San Francisco: Alemany Press, 1971.